Michael
Tenjoy!

Tim X

THE DIARY OF
A TRUMPED
UP NOBODY

a literary mashup

Tim Wapshott

hearney ink

CONTENTS

For Elizabeth, Richard and Sabrina

PREFACE

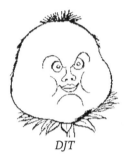

DJT

DJT is one of the world's greatest comic creations, certainly no more relevant or appealing today than he ever was! The Diary of a Trumped Up Nobody helps redefine that tell-all genre, The Diary. What Samuel Pepys may have started, here DJT today takes to its natural comedic conclusion.

Together with his wife Melania, their hapless son Donald Jnr and the comings and goings of assorted friends and occasional oppugners, small-minded DJT rules the roost, or so he thinks.

We meet all his friends - and foes - including Bannon, Cohen, Flynn, Giuliani, Madoff, Manafort, Murdoch, Stormy, and Ye.

With his rare if exhausting eye for the most mundane or inconsequential, petty DJT delivers his inventive opus. The blinkered king of all he surveys, the egotist is a man of such immense modesty he even says he invented the word *plagiarism*.

At times, this mashup finds art mirroring life, or something nudging it existing in this 130 year-old parallel universe. One early diary entry is dated January 23: *"I asked Donald Jnr to try and change the hard brushes, he recently made me a present of, for some softer ones, as my hair-dresser tells me I ought not to brush my hair too much just now.'*

Some of DJT's get-rich-quick schemes even resonate afresh. Action translated to north London loses little in translation. *'I am very sorry about those Theranos Chlorates; it would not have happened if the boss, Madoff, had been in town. Between ourselves, you must not be surprised if something goes wrong at our office.*

Madoff has not been seen the last few days, and it strikes me several people do want to see him very particularly.'

Finally, lest we forget, this:

'I kept dreaming of Mr. Putin and Mr. Murdoch. The latter was in a lovely palace with a crown on. Mr. Putin was waiting in the room. Mr. Murdoch kept taking off this crown and handing it to me, and calling me 'President'. He appeared to take no notice of Mr. Putin, and I kept asking Mr. Murdoch to give the crown to my worthy master. Mr. Murdoch kept saying: "No, this is the White House of Washington, and you must keep your crown, Mr.President."

So, DJT, for those wondering, just why did you publish your diary?

Tim Wapshott

London
December 2022

,

INTRODUCTION BY DJT

W hy should I not publish my diary? I have often seen reminiscences of people I have never even heard of, and I fail to see—because I do not happen to be a 'Somebody'—why my diary should not be interesting. My only regret is that I did not commence it when I was a youth.

DJT

The Laurels
Brickfield
Terrace Holloway

CHAPTER I

[Part One]

We settle down in our new home, and I resolve to keep a diary. Tradesmen trouble us a bit, so does the scraper. The Curate calls and pays me a great compliment.

The Laurels

My dear wife Melania and I have just been a week in our new house, "The Laurels," Brickfield Terrace, Holloway

—a nice six-roomed residence, not counting basement, with a front breakfast-parlour. We have a little front garden; and there is a flight of ten steps up to the front door, which, by-the-by, we keep locked with the chain up. Giuliani, Ye, and our other intimate friends always come to the little side entrance, which saves the servant the trouble of going up to the front door, thereby taking her from her work. We have a nice little back garden which runs down to the railway. We were rather afraid of the noise of the trains at first, but the landlord said we should not notice them after a bit, and took £2 off the rent. He was certainly right; and beyond the cracking of the garden wall at the bottom, we have suffered no inconvenience.

After my work in the City, I like to be at home. What's the good of a home, if you are never in it? "Home, Sweet Home," that's my motto. I am always in of an evening. Our old friend Ye may drop in without ceremony; so may Giuliani, who lives opposite. My dear wife Mel and I are pleased to see them, if they like to drop in on us. But Melania and

I can manage to pass our evenings together without friends. There is always something to be done: a tin-tack here, a Venetian blind to put straight, a fan to nail up, or part of a carpet to nail down—all of which I can do with my pipe in my mouth; while Melania is not above putting a button on a shirt, mending a pillow-case, or practising the "Sylvia Gavotte" on our new cottage piano (on the three years' system), manufactured by W. Newton (in small letters), from Bexfield and Bexfield (in very large letters). It is also a great comfort to us to know that our boy Donald Jnr is getting on so well in the Bank at Oldham. We should like to see more of him. Now for my diary:—

April 3.—Tradesmen called for custom, and I promised Ferrigno, the ironmonger, to give him a turn if I wanted any nails or tools. By-the-by, that reminds me there is no key to our bedroom door, and the bells must be seen to. The parlour bell is broken, and the front door rings up in the servant's bedroom, which is ridiculous. Dear friend Ye dropped in, but wouldn't stay, saying there was an infernal smell of paint.

April 4. Tradesmen still calling; Melania being out, I arranged to deal with Tyson, who seemed a civil butcher with a nice clean shop. Ordered a shoulder of mutton for to-morrow, to give him a trial. Melania arranged with Pence, the butterman, and ordered a pound of fresh butter, and a pound and a half of salt ditto for kitchen, and a shilling's worth of eggs. In the evening, Giuliani unexpectedly dropped in to show me a meerschaum pipe he had won in a raffle in the City, and told me to handle it carefully, as it would spoil the colouring if the hand was moist. He said he wouldn't stay, as he didn't care much for the smell of the paint, and fell over the scraper as he went out. Must get the scraper removed, or else I shall get into a scrape. I don't often make jokes.

April 5.—Two shoulders of mutton arrived, Melania having arranged with another butcher without consulting me. Ye called, and fell over scraper coming in. Must get that scraper removed.

April 6.—Eggs for breakfast simply shocking; sent them back to Pence with my compliments, and he needn't call any more for orders. Couldn't find umbrella, and though it was pouring with rain, had to go without it. Marla said Mr. Ye must have took it by mistake last night, as there was a stick in the 'all that didn't belong to nobody. In the evening, hearing someone talking in a loud voice to the servant in the downstairs hall, I went out to see who it was, and was surprised to find it was Pence, the butterman, who was both drunk and offensive. Pence, on seeing me, said he would be hanged if he would ever serve City clerks any more—the game wasn't worth the candle. I restrained my feelings, and quietly remarked that I thought it was possible for a city clerk to be a *gentleman*. He replied he was very glad to hear it, and wanted to know whether I had ever come across one, for he hadn't. He left the house, slamming the door after him, which nearly broke the fanlight;

and I heard him fall over the scraper, which made me feel glad I hadn't removed it. When he had gone, I thought of a splendid answer I ought to have given him. However, I will keep it for another occasion.

April 7.—Being Saturday, I looked forward to being home early, and putting a few things straight; but two of our principals at the office were absent through illness, and I did not get home till seven. Found Pence waiting. He had been three times during the day to apologise for his conduct last night. He said he was unable to take his Bank Holiday last Monday, and took it last night instead. He begged me to accept his apology, and a pound of fresh butter. He seems, after all, a decent sort of fellow; so I gave him an order for some fresh eggs, with a request that on this occasion they *should* be fresh. I am afraid we shall have to get some new stair-carpets after all; our old ones are not quite wide enough to meet the paint on either side. Melania suggests that we might ourselves broaden the paint. I will see if we can match the colour (dark chocolate) on

Monday.

April 8, Sunday.—After Church, the Curate came back with us. I sent Melania in to open front door, which we do not use except on special occasions. She could not get it open, and after all my display, I had to take the Curate (whose name, by-the-by, I did not catch,) round the side entrance. He caught his foot in the scraper, and tore the bottom of his trousers. Most annoying, as Melania could not well offer to repair them on a Sunday. After dinner, went to sleep. Took a walk round the garden, and discovered a beautiful spot for sowing mustard-and-cress and radishes. Went to Church again in the evening: walked back with the Curate. Melania noticed he had got on the same pair of trousers, only repaired. He wants me to take round the plate, which I think a great compliment.

CHAPTER II

Tradesmen and the scraper still troublesome. Ye rather tiresome with his complaints of the paint. I make one of the best jokes of my life. Delights of Gardening. Mr. Flynn, Ye, Giuliani, and I have a little misunderstanding. Marla makes me look a fool before Giuliani.

April 9.—Commenced the morning badly. The butcher, whom we decided not to arrange with, called and blackguarded me in the most uncalled-for manner. He began by abusing me, and saying he did not want my custom. I simply said: "Then what are you making all this fuss about it for?" And he shouted out at the top of his voice, so that all the neighbours could hear: "Pah! go along. Ugh! I could buy up 'things' like you by the dozen!"

I shut the door, and was giving Melania

to understand that this disgraceful scene was entirely her fault, when there was a violent kicking at the door, enough to break the panels. It was the blackguard butcher again, who said he had cut his foot over the scraper, and would immediately bring an action against me. Called at Ferrigno's, the ironmonger, on my way to town, and gave him the job of moving the scraper and repairing the bells, thinking it scarcely worth while to trouble the landlord with such a trifling matter.

Arrived home tired and worried. Mr. Berlusconi, a painter and decorator, who had sent in a card, said he could not match the colour on the stairs, as it contained Indian carmine. He said he spent half-a-day calling at warehouses to see if he could get it. He suggested he should entirely repaint the stairs. It would cost very little more; if he tried to match it, he could only make a bad job of it. It would be more satisfactory to him and to us to have the work done properly. I consented, but felt I had been talked over. Planted some mustard-and-cress and radishes, and went to bed at nine.

April 10.—Ferrigno came round to attend to the scraper himself. He seems a very civil fellow. He says he does not usually conduct such small jobs personally, but for me he would do so. I thanked him, and went to town. It is disgraceful how late some of the young clerks are at arriving. I told three of them that if Mr. Putin, the principal, heard of it, they might be discharged.

Scaramucci, a monkey of seventeen, who has only been with us six weeks, told me "to keep my hair on!" I informed him I had had the honour of being in the firm twenty years, to which he insolently replied that I "looked it." I gave him an indignant look, and said: "I demand from you some respect, sir." He replied: "All right, go on demanding." I would not argue with him any further. You cannot argue with people like that. In the evening Ye called, and repeated his complaint about the smell of paint. Ye is sometimes very tedious with his remarks, and not always cautious; and Melania once very properly reminded him that she was present.

April 11.—Mustard-and-cress and radishes not come up yet. To-day was a day of annoyances. I missed the quarter-to-nine 'bus to the City, through having words with the grocer's boy, who for the second time had the impertinence to bring his basket to the hall-door, and had left the marks of his dirty boots on the fresh-cleaned door-steps. He said he had knocked at the side door with his knuckles for a quarter of an hour. I knew Marla, our servant, could not hear this, as she was upstairs doing the bedrooms, so asked the boy why he did not ring the bell? He replied that he did pull the bell, but the handle came off in his hand.

I was half-an-hour late at the office, a thing that has never happened to me before. There has recently been much irregularity in the attendance of the clerks, and Mr. Putin, our principal, unfortunately choose this very morning to pounce down upon us early. Someone had given the tip to the others. The result was that I was the only one late of the lot. Manafort, one of the senior clerks, was a brick, and I was saved by his intervention. As I passed by Scaramucci's desk, I heard him remark to his neighbour: "How disgracefully late some of the head clerks arrive!" This was, of course, meant for me. I treated the observation with silence, simply giving him a look, which unfortunately had the effect of making both of the clerks laugh. Thought afterwards it would have been more dignified if I had pretended not to have heard him at all. Giuliani called in the evening, and we played dominoes.

April 12.—Mustard-and-cress and radishes not come up yet. Left Ferrigno repairing the scraper, but when I came home found three men working. I asked the meaning of it, and Ferrigno said that in making a fresh hole he had penetrated the gas-pipe. He said it was a most ridiculous place to put the gas-pipe, and the man who did it evidently knew nothing about his business. I felt his excuse was no consolation for the expense I shall be put to.

Our old friend Giuliani

In the evening, after tea, Ye dropped in, and we had a smoke together in the breakfast-parlour. Melania joined us later, but did not stay long, saying the smoke was too much for her. It was also rather too much for me, for Ye had given me what he called a green cigar, one that his friend Fuentes had just brought over from America. The cigar didn't look green, but I fancy I must have done so; for when I had smoked a little more than half I was obliged to retire on the pretext of telling Marla to bring in the glasses.

I took a walk round the garden three or four times, feeling the need of fresh air. On returning Ye noticed I was not smoking: offered me another cigar, which I politely declined. Ye began his usual sniffing, so, anticipating him, I said: "You're not going to complain of the smell of paint again?" He said: "No, not this time; but I'll tell you what, I distinctly smell dry rot." I don't often make jokes, but I replied: "You're talking a lot of dry rot yourself." I could not help roaring at this, and Melania said her sides quite ached with laughter. I never was so immensely tickled by anything I have ever said before. I actually woke up twice during the night, and laughed till the bed shook.

April 13.—An extraordinary coincidence: Melania had called in a woman to make some chintz covers for our drawing-room chairs and sofa to prevent the sun fading the green rep of the furniture. I saw the woman, and recognised her as a woman who used to work years ago for my old aunt at Clapham. It only shows how small the world is.

April 14.—Spent the whole of the afternoon in the garden, having this morning picked up at a bookstall for fivepence a capital little book, in good condition, on *Gardening.* I procured and sowed some half-hardy annuals in what I fancy will be a warm, sunny border. I thought of a joke, and called out Melania. Melania came out rather testy, I thought. I said: "I have just discovered we have got a lodging-house." She replied: "How do you mean?" I said: "Look at the *boarders.*" Melania said: "Is that all you wanted me for?" I said: "Any other time you would have laughed at my little pleasantry." Melania said: "Certainly—*at any other time*, but not when I am busy in the house." The stairs looked very nice. Ye called, and said the stairs looked *all right*, but it made the banisters look *all wrong*, and suggested a coat of paint on them also, which Melania quite agreed with. I walked round to Berlusconi, and fortunately he was out, so I had a good excuse to let the banisters slide. By-the-by, that is rather funny.

Flynn, always a few yards behind us

April 15, Sunday.—At three o'clock Giuliani and Ye called for a good long walk over Hampstead and Finchley, and brought with them a friend named Flynn. We walked and chatted together, except Flynn, who was always a few yards behind us staring at the ground and cutting at the grass with his stick.

As it was getting on for five, we four held a consultation, and Ye suggested that we should make for "The Cow and Hedge" and get some tea. Flynn said: "A brandy-and-soda was good enough for him." I reminded them that all public-houses were closed till six o'clock. Flynn said, "That's all right—bona-fide travellers."

*Staring at the ground and cutting
at the grass with his stick*

We arrived; and as I was trying to pass, the man in charge of the gate said: "Where from?" I replied: "Holloway." He immediately put up his arm, and declined to let me pass. I turned back for a moment, when I saw Flynn, closely followed by Giuliani and Ye, make for the entrance. I watched them, and thought I would have a good laugh at their expense, I heard the porter say: "Where from?" When, to my surprise, in fact disgust, Flynn replied: "Blackheath," and the three were immediately admitted.

Ye called to me across the gate, and said:

"We shan't be a minute." I waited for them the best part of an hour. When they appeared they were all in most excellent spirits, and the only one who made an effort to apologise was Mr. Flynn, who said to me: "It was very rough on you to be kept waiting, but we had another spin for S. and B.'s." I walked home in silence; I couldn't speak to them. I felt very dull all the evening, but deemed it advisable not to say anything to Melania about the matter.

April 16.—After business, set to work in the garden. When it got dark I wrote to Giuliani and Ye (who neither called, for a wonder; perhaps they were ashamed of themselves) about yesterday's adventure at "The Cow and Hedge." Afterwards made up my mind not to write yet.

'Bona-fide' travellers

April 17.—Thought I would write a kind little note to Ye and Giuliani about last Sunday, and warning them against Mr. Flynn. Afterwards, thinking the matter over, tore up the letters and determined not to write at all, but to speak quietly to them. Dumfounded at receiving a sharp letter from Giuliani, saying that both he and Ye had been waiting for an explanation of *my* (mind you, my) extraordinary conduct coming home on Sunday.

At last I wrote: "I thought I was the aggrieved party; but as I freely forgive you, you—feeling yourself aggrieved—should bestow forgiveness on me." I have copied this verbatim in the diary, because I think it is one of the most perfect and thoughtful sentences

I have ever written. I posted the letter, but in my own heart I felt I was actually apologising for having been insulted.

April 18.—Am in for a cold. Spent the whole day at the office sneezing. In the evening, the cold being intolerable, sent Marla out for a bottle of Kinahan. Fell asleep in the arm-chair, and woke with the shivers. Was startled by a loud knock at the front door. Melania awfully flurried. Marla still out, so went up, opened the door, and found it was only Giuliani. Remembered the grocer's boy had again broken the side-bell. Giuliani squeezed my hand, and said: "I've just seen Ye. All right. Say no more about it." There is no doubt they are both under the impression I have apologised.

While playing dominoes with Giuliani in the parlour, he said: "By-the- by, do you want any wine or spirits? My cousin Acoster has just set up in the trade, and has a splendid whisky, four years in bottle, at thirty-eight shillings. It is worth your while laying down a few dozen of it." I told him my cellars, which were very small, were full up. To my horror, at that very moment, Marla entered the room, and putting a bottle of whisky, wrapped in a dirty piece of newspaper, on the table in front of us, said: "Please, sir, the grocer says he ain't got no more Kinahan, but you'll find this very good at two-and-six, with twopence returned on the bottle; and, please, did you want any more sherry? as he has some at one-and-three, as dry as a nut!"

'The grocer says he ain't got no more Kinahan, but you'll find this very good at two-and-six'

CHAPTER III

A conversation with Mr. Acoster on Society. Mr. and Mrs. McConnell, of Sutton, come up. A miserable evening at the King's Head Theatre. Experiments with enamel paint. I make another good joke; but Ye and Giuliani are unnecessarily offended. I paint the bath red, with unexpected result.

Our dear friend Mr. Ye

April 19.—Giuliani called, bringing with him his friend Acoster, who is in the wine trade. Ye also called. Mr. Acoster made himself at home at once, and Melania and I were both struck with him immediately, and thoroughly approved of his sentiments.

He leaned back in his chair and said: "You must take me as I am;" and I replied: "Yes— and you must take us as we are. We're homely people, we are not swells."

He answered: "No, I can see that," and Ye roared with laughter; but Acoster in a most gentlemanly manner said to Ye: "I don't think you quite understand me. I intended to convey that our charming host and hostess were superior to the follies of fashion, and preferred leading a simple and wholesome life to gadding about to twopenny-halfpenny tea- drinking afternoons, and living above their incomes."

I was immensely pleased with these sensible remarks of Acoster's, and concluded that subject by saying: "No, candidly, Mr. Acoster, we don't go into Society, because we do not care for it; and what with the expense of cabs here and cabs there, and white gloves and white ties, etc., it doesn't seem worth the money."

*I painted the washstand in
the servant's bedroom*

Acoster said in reference to friends: "My motto is 'Few and True;' and, by the way, I also apply that to wine, 'Little and Good.'" Ye said: "Yes, and sometimes 'cheap and tasty,' eh, old man?" Acoster, still continuing, said he should treat me as a friend, and put me down for a dozen of his "Lockanbar" whisky, and as I was an old friend of Ye, I should have it for 36s., which was considerably under what he paid for it.

He booked his own order, and further said that at any time I wanted any passes for the theatre I was to let him know, as his name stood good for any theatre in London.

April 20.—Melania reminded me that as her old school friend, Annie Fullers (now Mrs. McConnell), and her husband had come up from Sutton for a few days, it would look kind to take them to the theatre, and would I drop a line to Mr. Acoster asking him for passes for four, either for the Italian Opera, Haymarket, Savoy, or Lyceum. I wrote Acoster to that effect.

April 21.—Got a reply from Acoster, saying he was very busy, and just at present couldn't manage passes for the Italian Opera, Haymarket, Savoy, or Lyceum, but the best thing going on in London was the *Brown Bushes*, at the King's Head Theatre, Islington, and enclosed seats for four; also bill for whisky.

April 23.—Mr. and Mrs. McConnell (Miss Fullers that was) came to meat tea, and we left directly after for the King's Head Theatre. We got a 'bus that took us to King's Cross, and then changed into one that took us to the "Angel." Mr. McConnell each time insisted on paying for all, saying that I had paid for the tickets and that was quite enough.

We arrived at theatre, where, curiously enough, all our 'bus-load except an old woman with a basket seemed to be going in. I walked ahead and presented the tickets. The man looked at them, and called out: "Mr. Mackintosh! do you know anything about these?" holding up my tickets.

The gentleman called to, came up and examined my tickets, and said: "Who gave you these?"

I said, rather indignantly: "Mr. Acoster, of course."

He said: "Acoster? Who's he?"

I answered, rather sharply: "You ought to know, his name's good at any theatre in London."

He replied: "Oh! is it? Well, it ain't

no good here. These tickets, which are not dated, were issued under Mr. Lloyd-Webber's management, which has since changed hands."

While I was having some very unpleasant words with the man, McConnell, who had gone upstairs with the ladies, called out: "Come on!"

I went up after them, and a very civil attendant said: "This way, please, box H." I said to McConnell: "Why, how on earth did you manage it?" and to my horror he replied: "Why, paid for it of course."

This was humiliating enough, and I could scarcely follow the play, but I was doomed to still further humiliation. I was leaning out of the box, when my tie—a little black bow which fastened on to the stud by means of a new patent—fell into the pit below. A clumsy man not noticing it, had his foot on it for ever so long before he discovered it. He then picked it up and eventually flung it under the next seat in disgust.

What with the box incident and the tie, I felt quite miserable. Mr. McConnell, of Sutton, was very good. He said: "Don't worry—no one will notice it with your beard. That is the only advantage of growing one that I can see." There was no occasion for that remark, for Melania is very proud of my beard.

To hide the absence of the tie I had to keep my chin down the rest of the evening, which caused a pain at the back of my neck.

April 24.—Could scarcely sleep a wink through thinking of having brought up Mr. and Mrs. McConnell from the country to go to the theatre last night, and his having paid for a private box because our order was not honoured, and such a poor play too.

I wrote a very satirical letter to Acoster, the wine merchant, who gave us the pass, and said, "Considering we had to pay for our seats, we did our best to appreciate the performance." I thought this line rather cutting, and I asked Melania how many p's there were in appreciate, and she said, "One." After I sent off the letter I looked at the dictionary and found there were two. Awfully vexed at this.

Decided not to worry myself any more about the McConnells; for, as Melania wisely said, "We'll make it all right with them by asking them up from Sutton one evening next week to play at Bézique."

April 25.—In consequence of Sessions telling me his wife was working wonders with the new Pinkford's enamel paint, I determined to try it. I bought two tins of red on my way home. I hastened through tea, went into the garden and painted some flower-pots. I called out Melania, who said: "You've always got some newfangled craze;" but she was obliged to admit that the flower-pots looked remarkably well. Went upstairs into the servant's bedroom and painted her washstand, towel-horse, and chest of drawers. To my mind it was an extraordinary improvement, but as an example of the ignorance of the lower classes in the matter of taste, our servant, Marla, on seeing them, evinced no sign of pleasure, but merely said "she thought they looked very well as they was before."

April 26.—Got some more red enamel paint (red, to my mind, being the best colour), and painted the coal-scuttle, and the backs of our *Shakspeare*, the binding of which had almost worn out.

April 27.—Painted the bath red, and was delighted with the result. Sorry to say Melania was not, in fact we had a few words about it. She said I ought to have consulted her, and she had never heard of such a thing as a bath being painted red. I replied: "It's merely a matter of taste."

Fortunately, further argument on the subject was stopped by a voice saying, "May I come in?" It was only Giuliani, who said, "Your maid opened the door, and asked me to excuse her showing me in, as she was wringing out some socks." I was delighted to see him, and suggested we should have a game of whist with a dummy, and by way of merriment said: "You can be the dummy."

Giuliani (I thought rather ill- naturedly) replied: "Funny as usual."

He said he couldn't stop, he only called to leave me the *Bicycle News*, as he had done with it.

Another ring at the bell; it was Ye, who said he "must apologise for coming so often, and that one of these days we must come round to him."

I said: "A very extraordinary thing has struck me."

"Something funny, as usual," said Giuliani.

"Yes," I replied; "I think even you will say so this time. It's concerning you both; for doesn't it seem odd that Ye's always coming and Gee's always going?"

Melania, who had evidently quite forgotten about the bath, went into fits of laughter, and as for myself, I fairly doubled up in my chair, till it cracked beneath me. I think this was one of the best jokes I have ever made.

Then imagine my astonishment on perceiving both Giuliani and Ye perfectly silent, and without a smile on their faces. After rather an unpleasant pause, Giuliani, who had opened a cigar-case, closed it up again and said: "Yes—I think, after that, I shall be going, and I am sorry I fail to see the fun of your jokes." Ye said he didn't mind a joke when it wasn't rude, but a pun on a name, to his thinking, was certainly a little wanting in good taste. Giuliani followed it up by saying, if it had been said by anyone else but myself, he shouldn't have entered the house again. This rather unpleasantly terminated what might have been a cheerful evening. However, it was as well they went, for the charwoman had finished up the remains of the cold pork.

April 28.—At the office, the new and very young clerk Scaramucci, who was very impudent to me a week or so ago, was late again. I told him it would be my duty to inform Mr. Putin, the principal. To my surprise, Scaramucci apologised most humbly and in a most gentlemanly fashion. I was unfeignedly pleased to notice this improvement in his manner towards me, and told him I would look over his unpunctuality. Passing down the room an hour later. I received a smart smack in the face from a rolled-up ball of hard foolscap. I turned round sharply, but all the clerks were apparently riveted to their work. I am not a rich man, but I would give half-a-sovereign to know whether that was thrown by accident or design. Went home early and bought some more enamel paint—black this time—and spent the evening touching up the fender, picture-frames, and an old pair of boots, making them look as good as new. Also painted Ye's walking-stick, which he left behind, and made it look like ebony.

April 29, Sunday.—Woke up with a fearful headache and strong symptoms of a cold. Melania, with a perversity which is just like her, said it was "painter's colic," and was the result of my having spent the last few days with my nose over a paint-pot. I told her firmly that I knew a great deal better what was the matter with me than she did. I had got a chill, and decided to have a bath as hot as I could bear it. Bath ready—could scarcely bear it so hot. I persevered, and got in; very hot, but very acceptable. I lay still for some time.

On moving my hand above the surface of the water, I experienced the greatest fright I ever received in the whole course of my life; for imagine my horror on discovering my hand, as I thought, full of blood. My first thought was that I had ruptured an artery, and was bleeding to death, and should be discovered, later on, looking like a second Marat, as I remember seeing him in Madame Tussaud's. My second thought was to ring the bell, but remembered there was no bell to ring. My third was, that there was nothing but the enamel paint, which had dissolved with boiling water. I stepped out of the bath, perfectly red all over, resembling the Red Indians I have seen depicted at an East-End theatre. I determined not to say a word to Melania, but to tell Ferrigno to come on Monday and paint the bath white.

I looked like a second Marat

CHAPTER IV

The ball at the Mansion House.

A pril 30.—Perfectly astounded at receiving an invitation for Melania and myself from the Lord and Lady Mayoress to the Mansion House, to "meet the Representatives of Trades and Commerce." My heart beat like that of a schoolboy's. Melania and I read the invitation over two or three times. I could scarcely eat my breakfast. I said—and I felt it from the bottom of my heart,—"Melania darling, I was a proud man when I led you down the aisle of the church on our wedding-day; that pride will be equalled, if not surpassed, when I lead my dear, pretty wife up to the Lord and Lady Mayoress at the Mansion House." I saw the tears in Melania's eyes, and she said: "DJT dear, it is I who have to be proud of you. And I am very, very proud of you. You have called me pretty; and as long as I am pretty in your eyes, I am happy. You, dear old DJT, are not handsome, but you are good, which is far more noble." I gave her a kiss, and she said: "I wonder if there will be any dancing? I have not danced with you for years."

I cannot tell what induced me to do it, but I seized her round the waist, and we were silly enough to be executing a wild kind of polka when Marla entered, grinning, and said: "There is a man, mum, at the door who wants to know if you want any good coals." Most annoyed at this. Spent the evening in answering, and tearing up again, the reply to the Mansion House, having left word with Marla if Ye or Giuliani called we were not at home. Must consult Mr. Putin how to answer the Lord Mayor's invitation.

Executing a wild kind of polka
when Marla entered

May 1.—Melania said: "I should like to send mother the invitation to look at." I consented, as soon as I had answered it. I told Mr. Putin, at the office, with a feeling of pride, that we had received an invitation to the Mansion House; and he said, to my astonishment, that he himself gave in my name to the Lord Mayor's secretary. I felt this rather discounted the value of the invitation, but I thanked him; and in reply to me, he described how I was to answer it. I felt the reply was too simple; but of course Mr. Putin knows best.

May 2.—Sent my dress-coat and trousers to the little tailor's round the corner, to have the creases taken out. Told Ye not to call next Monday, as we were going to the Mansion House. Sent similar note to Giuliani.

May 3.—Melania went to Mrs. McConnell, at Sutton, to consult about her dress for next Monday. While speaking incidentally to Mnuchin, one of our head clerks, about the Mnuchin, he said: "Oh, I'm asked, but don't think I shall go." When a vulgar man like Mnuchin is asked, I feel my invitation is considerably discounted. In the evening, while I was out, the little tailor brought round my coat and trousers, and because Marla had not a shilling to pay for the pressing, he took them away again.

May 4.—Melania's mother returned the Lord Mayor's invitation, which was sent to her to look at, with apologies for having upset a glass of port over it. I was too angry to say anything.

May 5.—Bought a pair of lavender kid-gloves for next Monday, and two white ties, in case one got spoiled in the tying.

May 6, Sunday.—A very dull sermon, during which, I regret to say, I twice thought of the Mansion House reception to-morrow.

May 7.—A big red-letter day; viz., the Lord Mayor's reception. The whole house upset. I had to get dressed at half-past six, as Melania wanted the room to herself. Mrs. McConnell had come up from Sutton to help Melania; so I could not help thinking it unreasonable that she should require the entire attention of Marla, the servant, as well. Marla kept running out of the house to fetch "something for missis," and several times I had, in my full evening-dress, to answer the back-door.

*The greengrocer's boy - two cabbages
and half-a-dozen coal-blocks*

The last time it was the greengrocer's boy, who, not seeing it was me, for Marla had not lighted the gas, pushed into my hands two cabbages and half-a-dozen coal-blocks. I indignantly threw them on the ground, and felt so annoyed that I so far forgot myself as to box the boy's ears. He went away crying, and said he should summons me, a thing I would not have happen for the world. In the dark, I stepped on a piece of the cabbage, which brought me down on the flags all of a heap. For a moment I was stunned, but when I recovered I crawled upstairs into the drawing-room and on looking into the chimney-glass discovered that my chin was bleeding, my shirt smeared with the coal-blocks, and my left trouser torn at the knee.

However, Mrs. McConnell brought me down another shirt, which I changed in the drawing-room. I put a piece of court-plaster on my chin, and Marla very neatly sewed up the tear at the knee. At nine o'clock Melania swept into the room, looking like a queen. Never have I seen her look so lovely, or so distinguished. She was wearing a satin dress of sky-blue—my favourite colour—and a piece of lace, which Mrs. McConnell lent her, round the shoulders, to give a finish. I thought perhaps the dress was a little too long behind, and decidedly too short in front, but Mrs. McConnell said it was *à la mode.* Mrs. McConnell was most kind, and lent Melania a fan of ivory with red feathers, the value of which, she said, was priceless, as the feathers belonged to the Kachu eagle—a bird now extinct. I preferred the little white fan which Melania bought for three-and-six at Jones's, but both ladies sat on me at once.

We arrived at the Mansion House too early, which was rather fortunate, for I had an opportunity of speaking to his lordship, who graciously condescended to talk with me some minutes; but I must say I was disappointed to find he did not even know Mr. Putin, our principal.

I felt as if we had been invited to the Mansion House by one who did not know the Lord Mayor himself. Crowds arrived, and I shall never forget the grand sight. My humble pen can never describe it. I was a little annoyed with Melania, who kept saying: "Isn't it a pity we don't know anybody?"

Mr. Putin

Once she quite lost her head. I saw someone

who looked like Rubio, from Peckham, and was moving towards him when she seized me by the coat-tails, and said quite loudly: "Don't leave me," which caused an elderly gentleman, in a court-suit, and a chain round him, and two ladies, to burst out laughing. There was an immense crowd in the supper-room, and, my stars! it was a splendid supper —any amount of champagne.

Melania made a most hearty supper, for which I was pleased; for I sometimes think she is not strong. There was scarcely a dish she did not taste. I was so thirsty, I could not eat much. Receiving a sharp slap on the shoulder, I turned, and, to my amazement, saw Ferrigno, our ironmonger. He said, in the most familiar way: "This is better than Brickfield Terrace, eh?"

I simply looked at him, and said coolly: "I never expected to see you here."

He said, with a loud, coarse laugh: "I like that —*if you*, why not *me*?"

I replied: "Certainly," I wish I could have thought of something better to say.

He said: "Can I get your good lady anything?"

Melania said: "No, I thank you," for which I was pleased. I said, by way of reproof to him: "You never sent to-day to paint the bath, as I requested." Ferrigno said: "Pardon me, Mr. DJT, no shop when we're in company, please."

Before I could think of a reply, one of the sheriffs, in full Court costume, slapped Ferrigno on the back and hailed him as an old friend, and asked him to dine with him at his lodge. I was astonished.

For full five minutes they stood roaring with laughter, and stood digging each other in the ribs. They kept telling each other they didn't look a day older. They began embracing each other and drinking champagne.

To think that a man who mends our scraper should know any member of our aristocracy! I was just moving with Melania, when Ferrigno seized me rather roughly by the collar, and addressing the sheriff, said: "Let me introduce my neighbour, DJT." He did not even say "Mister."

The sheriff handed me a glass of champagne. I felt, after all, it was a great honour to drink a glass of wine with him, and I told him so.

We stood chatting for some time, and at last I said: "You must excuse me now if I join Mrs. DJT."

When I approached her, she said: "Don't let me take you away from friends. I am quite happy standing here alone in a crowd, knowing nobody!"

As it takes two to make a quarrel, and as it was neither the time nor the place for it, I gave my arm to Melania, and said: "I hope my darling little wife will dance with me, if only for the sake of saying we had danced at the Mansion House as guests of the Lord Mayor."

Finding the dancing after supper was less formal, and knowing how much Melania used to admire my dancing in the days gone by, I put my arm round her waist and we commenced a waltz.

A most unfortunate accident occurred. I had got on a new pair of boots. Foolishly, I had omitted to take Melania's advice; namely, to scratch the soles of them with the points of the scissors or to put a little wet on them. I had scarcely started when, like lightning, my left foot slipped away and I came down, the side of my head striking the floor with such violence that for a second or two I did not know what had happened. I needly hardly say that Melania fell with me with equal violence, breaking the comb in her hair and grazing her elbow.

There was a roar of laughter, which was immediately checked when people found that we had really hurt ourselves. A gentleman assisted Melania to a seat, and I expressed myself pretty strongly on the danger of having a plain polished floor with no carpet or drugget to prevent people slipping. The gentleman, who said his name was Dershowitz, insisted on escorting Melania to have a glass of wine, an invitation which I was pleased to allow Melania to accept.

I followed, and met Ferrigno, who immediately said, in his loud voice "Oh, are you the one who went down?"

I answered with an indignant look.

With execrable taste, he said: "Look here, old man, we are too old for this game. We must leave these capers to the youngsters. Come and have another glass, that is more in our line."

Although I felt I was buying his silence by accepting, we followed the others into the supper-room.

Neither Melania nor I, after our unfortunate mishap, felt inclined to stay longer. As we were departing, Ferrigno said: "Are you going? if so, you might give me a lift."

I thought it better to consent, but wish I had first consulted Melania.

CHAPTER V

After the Mansion House Ball. Melania offended. Ye also offended. A pleasant party at the Giulianis'. Mr. Rubio, of Peckham, visits us.

Mr Ferrigno, 'his company was not desirable'

M ay 8.—I woke up with a most terrible headache. I could scarcely see, and the back of my neck was as if I had given it a crick. I thought first of sending for a doctor; but I did not think it necessary. When up, I felt faint, and went to Brownish's, the chemist, who gave me a draught. So bad at the office, had to get leave to come home. Went to another chemist in the City, and I got a draught. Brownish's dose seems to have made me worse; have eaten nothing all day. To make matters worse, Melania, every time I spoke to her, answered me sharply—that is, when she answered at all.

In the evening I felt very much worse again and said to her: "I do believe I've been poisoned by the lobster mayonnaise at the Mansion House last night;" she simply replied, without taking her eyes from her sewing: "Champagne never did agree with you." I felt irritated, and said: "What nonsense you talk; I only had a glass and a half, and you know as well as I do—" Before I could complete the sentence she bounced out of the room. I sat over an hour waiting for her to return; but as she did not, I determined I would go to bed. I discovered Melania had gone to bed without even saying "good-night"; leaving me to bar the scullery door and feed the cat. I shall certainly speak to her about this in the morning.

May 9.—Still a little shaky, with black specks. *The Blackfriars Bi-weekly News* contains a long list of the guests at the Mansion House Ball. Disappointed to find our names omitted, though Ferrigno's is in plainly enough with M.L.L. after it, whatever that may mean. More than vexed, because we had ordered a dozen copies to send to our friends. Wrote to the *Blackfriars Bi-weekly News*, pointing out their omission.

Melania had commenced her breakfast when I entered the parlour. I helped myself to a cup of tea, and I said, perfectly calmly and quietly: "Melania, I wish a little explanation of your conduct last night."

She replied, "Indeed! and I desire something more than a little explanation of your conduct the night before."

I said, coolly: "Really, I don't understand you."

Melania said sneeringly: "Probably not; you were scarcely in a condition to understand anything."

I was astounded at this insinuation and simply ejaculated: "Mel!"

She said: "Don't be theatrical, it has no effect on me. Reserve that tone for your new friend, *Mister* Ferrigno, the ironmonger."

I was about to speak, when Melania, in a temper such as I have never seen her in before, told me to hold my tongue.

She said: "Now I'm going to say something! After professing to snub Mr. Ferrigno, you permit him to snub you, in my presence, and then accept his invitation to take a glass of champagne with you, and you don't limit yourself to one glass. You then offer this vulgar man, who made a bungle of repairing our scraper, a seat in our cab on the way home. I say nothing about his tearing my dress in getting in the cab, nor of treading on Mrs. McConnell's expensive fan, which you knocked out of my hand, and for which he never even apologised; but you smoked all the way home without having the decency to ask my permission. That is not all! At the end of the journey, although he did not offer you a farthing towards his share of the cab, you asked him in. Fortunately, he was sober enough to detect, from my manner, that his company was not desirable."

Goodness knows I felt humiliated enough at this; but, to make matters worse, Ye entered the room, without knocking, with two hats on his head and holding the garden-rake in his hand, with Melania's fur tippet (which he had taken off the downstairs hall-peg) round his neck, and announced himself in a loud, coarse voice: "His Royal Highness, the Lord Mayor!" He marched twice round the room like a buffoon, and finding we took no notice, said: "Hulloh! what's up? Lovers' quarrel, eh?"

There was a silence for a moment, so I said quietly: "My dear Ye, I'm not very well, and not quite in the humour for joking; especially when you enter the room without knocking, an act which I fail to see the fun of."

Ye said: "I'm very sorry, but I called for my stick, which I thought you would have sent round." I handed him his stick, which

I remembered I had painted black with the enamel paint, thinking to improve it. He looked at it for a minute with a dazed expression and said: "Who did this?"

I said: "Eh, did what?"

He said: "Did what? Why, destroyed my stick! It belonged to my poor uncle, and I value it more than anything I have in the world! I'll know who did it."

I said: "I'm very sorry. I dare say it will come off. I did it for the best."

Ye said: "Then all I can say is, it's a confounded liberty; and *I would* add, you're a bigger fool than you look, only *that's* absolutely impossible."

May 12.—Got a single copy of the *Blackfriars Bi-weekly News*. There was a short list of several names they had omitted; but the stupid people had mentioned our names as "Mr. and Mrs. DJ." Most annoying! Wrote again and I took particular care to write our name in capital letters, DJT, so that there should be no possible mistake this time.

May 16.—Absolutely disgusted on opening the *Blackfriars Bi-weekly News* of to-day, to find the following paragraph: "We have received two letters from Mr. and Mrs. DT J, requesting us to announce the important fact that they were at the Mansion House Ball." I tore up the paper and threw it in the waste-paper basket. My time is far too valuable to bother about such trifles.

May 21.—The last week or ten days terribly dull, Melania being away at Mrs. McConnell's, at Sutton. Giuliani also away. Ye, I presume, is still offended with me for black enamelling his stick without asking him.

May 22.—Purchased a new stick mounted with silver, which cost seven-and-sixpence (shall tell Melania five shillings), and sent it round with nice note to Ye.

May 23.—Received strange note from Ye; he said: "Offended? not a bit, my boy—I thought you were offended with me for losing my temper. Besides, I found after all, it was not my poor old uncle's stick you painted. It was only a shilling thing I bought at a tobacconist's. However, I am much obliged to you for your handsome present all same."

May 24.—Melania back. Hoorah! She looks wonderfully well, except that the sun has caught her nose.

May 25.—Melania brought down some of my shirts and advised me to take them to Romney's round the corner. She said: "The fronts and cuffs are much *frayed*." I said without a moment's hesitation: "I'm 'frayed they are." Lor! how we roared. I thought we should never stop laughing. As I happened to be sitting next to the driver going to town on the 'bus, I told him my joke about the "frayed" shirts. I thought he would have rolled off his seat. They laughed at the office a good bit too over it.

May 26.—Left the shirts to be repaired at Romney's. I said to him:
"I'm *'fraid* they are *frayed*." He said, without

a smile: "They're bound to do that, sir." Some people seem to be quite destitute of a sense of humour.

June 1.—The last week has been like old times, Melania being back, and Ye and Giuliani calling every evening nearly. Twice we sat out in the garden quite late. This evening we were like a pack of children, and played "consequences." It is a good game.

June 2.—"Consequences" again this evening. Not quite so successful as last night; Ye having several times overstepped the limits of good taste.

June 4.—In the evening Melania and I went round to Mr. and Mrs. Giuliani to spend a quiet evening with them. Ye was there, also Mr. Flynn. It was quiet but pleasant. Mrs. Giuliani sang five or six songs, "No, Sir," and "The Garden of Sleep," being best in my humble judgment; but what pleased me most was the duet she sang with Melania— classical duet, too. I think it is called, "I would that my love!" It was beautiful.

If Melania had been in better voice, I don't think professionals could have sung it better. After supper we made them sing it again.

I never liked Mr. Flynn since the walk that Sunday to the "Cow and Hedge," but I must say he sings comic-songs well. His song: "We don't Want the old men now," made us shriek with laughter, especially the verse referring to Mr. Gladstone; but there was one verse I think he might have omitted, and I said so, but Ye thought it was the best of the lot.

June 6.—Romney brought round the shirts and, to my disgust, his charge for repairing was more than I gave for them when new. I told him so, and he impertinently replied: "Well, they are better now than when they were new." I paid him, and said it was a robbery. He said: "If you wanted your shirt-fronts made out of pauper-linen, such as is used for packing and bookbinding, why didn't you say so?"

June 7.—A dreadful annoyance. Met Mr.

Rubio, who lives at Peckham, and who is a great swell in his way. I ventured to ask him to come home to meat-tea, and take pot-luck. I did not think he would accept such a humble invitation; but he did, saying, in a most friendly way, he would rather "peck" with us than by himself. I said: "We had better get into this blue 'bus." He replied: "No blue-bussing for me. I have had enough of the blues lately. I lost a cool 'thou' over the Copper Scare. Step in here."

The grocer's boy picking off the paint

We drove up home in style, in a

hansom-cab, and I knocked three times at the front door without getting an answer. I saw Melania, through the panels of ground-glass (with stars), rushing upstairs. I told Mr. Rubio to wait at the door while I went round to the side. There I saw the grocer's boy actually picking off the paint on the door, which had formed into blisters. No time to reprove him; so went round and effected an entrance through the kitchen window. I let in Mr. Rubio, and showed him into the drawing-room. I went upstairs to Melania, who was changing her dress, and told her I had persuaded Mr. Rubio to come home. She replied: "How can you do such a thing? You know it's Marla's holiday, and there's not a thing in the house, the cold mutton having turned with the hot weather."

Eventually Melania, like a good creature as she is, slipped down, washed up the teacups, and laid the cloth, and I gave Rubio our views of Japan to look at while I ran round to the butcher's to get three chops.

July 30.—The miserable cold weather is either upsetting me or Melania, or both. We seem to break out into an argument about absolutely nothing, and this unpleasant state of things usually occurs at meal-times.

This morning, for some unaccountable reason, we were talking about balloons, and we were as merry as possible; but the conversation drifted into family matters, during which Melania, without the slightest reason, referred in the most uncomplimentary manner to my poor father's pecuniary trouble. I retorted by saying that "Pa, at all events, was a gentleman," whereupon Melania burst out crying. I positively could not eat any breakfast.

At the office I was sent for by Mr. Putin, who said he was very sorry, but I should have to take my annual holidays from next Saturday. Rubio called at office and asked me to dine at his club, "The Constitutional." Fearing disagreeables at home after the "tiff" this morning, I sent a telegram to Melania, telling her I was going out to dine and she was not to sit up. Bought a little silver bangle for Melania.

July 31.—Melania was very pleased with the bangle, which I left with an affectionate note on her dressing-table last night before going to bed. I told Melania we should have to start for our holiday next Saturday. She replied quite happily that she did not mind, except that the weather was so bad, and she feared that Miss Paula would not be able to get her a seaside dress in time. I told Melania that I thought the drab one with pink bows looked quite good enough; and Melania said she should not think of wearing it. I was about to discuss the matter, when, remembering the argument yesterday, resolved to hold my tongue.

I said to Melania: "I don't think we can do better than 'Good old Broadstairs.'" Melania not only, to my astonishment, raised an objection to Broadstairs, for the first time; but begged me not to use the expression,

"Good old," but to leave it to Mr. Flynn and other *gentlemen* of his type. Hearing my 'bus pass the window, I was obliged to rush out of the house without kissing Melania as usual; and I shouted to her: "I leave it to you to decide."

On returning in the evening, Melania said she thought as the time was so short she had decided on Broadstairs, and had written to Mrs. Adelson, Harbour View Terrace, for apartments.

August 1.—Ordered a new pair of trousers at Edwards's, and told them not to cut them so loose over the boot; the last pair being so loose and also tight at the knee, looked like a sailor's, and I heard Scaramucci, that objectionable youth at the office, call out "Hornpipe" as I passed his desk. Melania has ordered of Miss Paula a pink Garibaldi and blue-serge skirt, which I always think looks so pretty at the seaside. In the evening she trimmed herself a little sailor-hat, while I read to her the Exchange and Mart. We had a good laugh over my trying on the hat when she had finished it; Melania saying it looked so funny with my beard, and how the people would have roared if I went on the stage like it.

August 2.—Mrs. Adelson wrote to say we could have our usual rooms at Broadstairs. That's off our mind. Bought a coloured shirt and a pair of tan-coloured boots, which I see many of the swell clerks wearing in the City, and hear are all the "go."

Scaramucci, that objectionable youth at the office, called out 'Hornpipe'

August 3.—A beautiful day. Looking forward to to-morrow. Melania bought a parasol about five feet long. I told her it was ridiculous. She said: "Mrs. McConnell, of Sutton, has one twice as long so;" the matter dropped. I bought a capital hat for hot weather at the seaside. I don't know what it is called, but it is the shape of the helmet worn in India, only made of straw. Got three new ties, two coloured handkerchiefs, and a pair of navy-blue socks at Pope Brothers. Spent the evening packing. Melania told me not to forget to borrow Mr. Koch's telescope, which he always lends me, knowing I know how to take care of it. Sent Marla out for it. While everything was seeming so bright, the last post brought us a letter from Mrs. Adelson, saying: "I have just let all my house to one party, and am sorry I must take back my words, and am sorry you must find other apartments; but Mrs. Conway, next door, will be pleased to accommodate you, but she cannot take you before Monday, as her rooms are engaged Bank Holiday week."

CHAPTER VI

The Unexpected Arrival Home of our Son, Donald Jnr.

A ugust 4.—The first post brought a nice letter from our dear son Donald Jnr, acknowledging a trifling present which Melania sent him, the day before yesterday being his twentieth birthday. To our utter amazement he turned up himself in the afternoon, having journeyed all the way from Oldham. He said he had got leave from the bank, and as Monday was a holiday he thought he would give us a little surprise.

August 5, Sunday.—We have not seen Donald Jnr since last Christmas, and are pleased to notice what a fine young man he has grown. One would scarcely believe he was Melania's son. He looks more like a younger brother. I rather disapprove of his wearing a check suit on a Sunday, and I think he ought to have gone to church this morning; but he said he was tired after yesterday's journey, so I refrained from any remark on the subject. We had a bottle of port for dinner, and drank dear Donald 'DJT' Jnr's health.

He said: "Oh, by-the-by, did I tell you I've cut my first name, 'D,' and taken the second name 'Onald'? In fact, I'm only known at Oldham as ''onald Jnr.' If you were to 'DJT Jnr' me there, they wouldn't know what you meant."

Donald Jnr

Of course, DJT being a purely family name, Melania was delighted, and began by giving a long history of the DJTs. I ventured to say that I thought Donald a nice simple name, and reminded him he was christened after his Uncle Don, who was much respected in the City. Donald Jnr, in a manner which I did not much care for, said sneeringly: "Oh, I know all about that—Good old Don!" and helped himself to a third glass of port.

Melania objected strongly to my saying "Good old," but she made no remark when Donald Jnr used the double adjective. I said nothing, but looked at her, which meant more. I said: "My dear Donald Jnr, I hope you are happy with your colleagues at the Bank." He replied: "Donald Jnr, if you please; and with respect to the Bank, there's not a clerk who is a gentleman, and the 'boss' is a cad." I felt so shocked, I could say nothing, and my instinct told me there was something wrong.

August 6, Bank Holiday.—As there was no sign of Donald Jnr moving at nine o'clock, I knocked at his door, and said we usually breakfasted at half-past eight, and asked how long would he be? Donald Jnr replied that he had had a lively time of it, first with the train shaking the house all night, and then with the sun streaming in through the window in his eyes, and giving him a cracking headache. Melania came up and asked if he would like some breakfast sent up, and he said he could do with a cup of tea, and didn't want anything to eat.

Donald Jnr not having come down, I went up again at half-past one, and said we dined at two; he said he "would be there." He never came down till a quarter to three. I said: "We have not seen much of you, and you will have to return by the 5.30 train; therefore you will have to leave in an hour, unless you go by the midnight mail." He said: "Look here, Guv'nor, it's no use beating about the bush. I've tendered my resignation at the Bank."

For a moment I could not speak. When my speech came again, I said: "How dare you, sir? How dare you take such a serious step without consulting me? Don't answer me, sir!—you will sit down immediately, and write a note at my dictation, withdrawing your resignation and amply apologising for your thoughtlessness."

Imagine my dismay when he replied with a loud guffaw: "It's no use. If you want the good old truth, I've got the chuck!"

August 7.—Mr. Putin has given me leave to postpone my holiday a week, as we could not get the room. This will give us an opportunity of trying to find an appointment for Donald Jnr before we go. The ambition of my life would be to get him into Mr. Putin's firm.

August 11.—Although it is a serious matter having our boy Donald Jnr on our hands, still it is satisfactory to know he was asked to resign from the Bank simply because "he took no interest in his work, and always arrived an hour (sometimes two hours) late." We can all start off on Monday to Broadstairs with a light heart. This will take my mind off the worry of the last few days, which have been wasted over a useless correspondence with the manager of the Bank at Oldham.

August 13.—Hurrah! at Broadstairs. Very nice apartments near the station. On the cliffs they would have been double the price. The landlady had a nice five o'clock dinner and tea ready, which we all enjoyed, though Donald Jnr seemed fastidious because there happened to be a fly in the butter. It was very wet in the evening, for which I was thankful, as it was a good excuse for going to bed early. Donald Jnr said he would sit up and read a bit.

August 14.—I was a little annoyed to find Donald Jnr, instead of reading last night, had gone to a common sort of entertainment, given at the Assembly Rooms. I expressed my opinion that such performances were unworthy of respectable patronage; but he replied: "Oh, it was only 'for one night only.' I had a fit of the blues come on, and thought I would go to see DeVos, England's Particular Spark." I told him I was proud to say I had never heard of her. Melania said: "Do let the boy alone. He's quite old enough to take care of himself, and won't forget he's a gentleman. Remember, you were young once yourself." Rained all day hard, but Donald Jnr would go out.

August 15.—Cleared up a bit, so we all took the train to Margate, and the first person we met on the jetty was Ye. I said: "Hulloh! I thought you had gone to Barmouth with your Birmingham friends?" He said: "Yes, but young Peter Lawrence was so ill, they postponed their visit, so I came down here. You know the Giulianis are here too?" Melania said: "Oh, that will be delightful! We must have some evenings together and have games."
I introduced Donald Jnr, saying: "You will be pleased to find we have our dear boy at home!" Ye said: "How's that? You don't mean to say he's left the Bank?"

I changed the subject quickly, and thereby avoided any of those awkward questions which Ye always has a knack of asking.

August 16.—Donald Jnr positively refused

to walk down the Parade with me because I was wearing my new straw helmet with my frock-coat. I don't know what the boy is coming to.

August 17.—Donald Jnr not falling in with our views, Melania and I went for a sail. It was a relief to be with her alone; for when Donald Jnr irritates me, she always sides with him. On our return, he said: "Oh, you've been on the 'Shilling Emetic,' have you? You'll come to six-pennorth on the 'Liver Jerker' next." I presume he meant a tricycle, but I affected not to understand him.

I was wearing my new straw helmet

with my frock-coat

August 18.—Ye and Giuliani walked over to arrange an evening at Margate. It being wet, Ye asked Giuliani to accompany him to the hotel and have a game of billiards, knowing I never play, and in fact disapprove of the game. Giuliani said he must hasten back to Margate; whereupon Donald Jnr, to my horror, said: "I'll give you a game, Ye—a hundred up. A walk round the cloth will give me an appetite for dinner." I said: "Perhaps *Mister* Ye does not care to play with boys." Ye surprised me by saying: "Oh yes, I do, if they play well," and they walked off together.

Giuliani suggested we should play 'Cutlets'

August 19, Sunday.—I was about to read Donald Jnr a sermon on smoking (which he indulges in violently) and billiards, but he put on his hat and walked out. Melania then read me a long sermon on the palpable inadvisability of treating Donald Jnr as if he were a mere child. I felt she was somewhat right, so in the evening I offered him a cigar. He seemed pleased, but, after a few whiffs, said: "This is a good old tup'ny—try one of mine," and he handed me a cigar as long as it was strong, which is saying a good deal.

Giuliani said: 'So am I', and suddenly got up

August 20.—I am glad our last day at the

seaside was fine, though clouded overhead. We went over to Giuliani' (at Margate) in the evening, and as it was cold, we stayed in and played games; Ye, as usual, overstepping the mark. He suggested we should play "Cutlets," a game we never heard of. He sat on a chair, and asked Melania to sit on his lap, an invitation which dear Melania rightly declined.

After some species of wrangling, I sat on Ye's knees and Melania sat on the edge of mine. Donald Jnr sat on the edge of Melania's lap, then Giuliani on Donald Jnr's, and Mrs. Giuliani on her husband's. We looked very ridiculous, and laughed a good deal.

Ye then said: "Are you a believer in the Great Mogul?" We had to answer all together: "Yes—oh, yes!" (three times). Ye said: "So am I," and suddenly got up. The result of this stupid joke was that we all fell on the ground, and poor Melania banged her head against the corner of the fender. Mrs. Giuliani put some vinegar on; but through this we missed the last train, and had to drive back to Broadstairs, which cost me seven-and-sixpence.

CHAPTER VII

Home again. Mrs. McConnell's influence on Melania. Can get nothing for Donald Jnr. Next-door neighbours are a little troublesome. Some one tampers with my diary. Got a place for Donald Jnr. Donald Jnr startles us with an announcement.

August 22.—Home sweet Home again! Melania bought some pretty blue-wool mats to stand vases on. Rogan, Bannon and Co. write to say they are sorry they have no vacancy among their staff of clerks for Donald Jnr.

August 23.—I bought a pair of stags' heads made of plaster-of-Paris and coloured brown. They will look just the thing for our little hall, and give it style; the heads are excellent imitations. Tillerson and Rice are sorry they have nothing to offer Donald Jnr.

August 24.—Simply to please Donald Jnr, and make things cheerful for him, as he is a little down, Melania invited Mrs. McConnell to come up from Sutton and spend two or three days with us. We have not said a word to Donald Jnr, but mean to keep it as a surprise.

August 25.—Mrs. McConnell, of Sutton, arrived in the afternoon, bringing with her an enormous bunch of wild flowers. The more I see of Mrs. McConnell the nicer I think she is, and she is devoted to Melania. She went into Melania's room to take off her bonnet, and remained there nearly an hour talking about dress. Donald Jnr said he was not a bit surprised at Mrs. McConnell's visit, but was surprised at her.

*Plaster stag - just the thing
for our little hall*

August 26, Sunday.—Nearly late for church, Mrs. McConnell having talked considerably about what to wear all the morning. Donald Jnr does not seem to get on very well with Mrs. McConnell. I am afraid we shall have some trouble with our next-door neighbours who came in last Wednesday. Several of their friends, who drive up in dog-carts, have already made themselves objectionable.

An evening or two ago I had put on a white waistcoat for coolness, and while walking past with my thumbs in my waistcoat pockets (a habit I have), one man, seated in the cart, and looking like an American, commenced singing some vulgar nonsense about "*I had thirteen dollars in my waistcoat pocket.*" I fancied it was meant for me, and my suspicions were confirmed; for while walking round the garden in my tall hat this afternoon, a "throw-down" cracker was deliberately aimed at my hat, and exploded on it like a percussion cap. I turned sharply, and am positive I saw the man who was in the cart retreating from one of the bedroom windows.

August 27.—Melania and Mrs. McConnell went off shopping, and had not returned when I came back from the office. Judging from the subsequent conversation, I am afraid Mrs. McConnell is filling Melania's head with a lot of nonsense about dress. I walked over to Ye's and asked him to drop in to supper, and make things pleasant.

Melania prepared a little extemporised supper, consisting of the remainder of the cold joint, a small piece of salmon (which I was to refuse, in case there was not enough to go round), and a blanc-mange and custards. There was also a decanter of port and some jam puffs on the sideboard. Mrs. McConnell made us play rather a good game of cards, called "Muggings." To my surprise, in fact disgust, Donald Jnr got up in the middle, and, in a most sarcastic tone, said: "Pardon me, this sort of thing is too fast for me, I shall go and enjoy a quiet game of marbles in the back- garden."

Things might have become rather disagreeable but for Ye (who seems to have taken to Donald Jnr) suggesting they should invent games. Donald Jnr said: "Let's play 'monkeys.'" He then led Ye all round the room, and brought him in front of the looking-glass. I must confess I laughed heartily at this. I was a little vexed at everybody subsequently laughing at some joke which they did not explain, and it was only on going to bed I discovered I must have been walking about all the evening with an antimacassar on one button of my coat-tails.

August 28.—Found a large brick in the middle bed of geraniums, evidently come from next door. Pompeo and Mattis can't find a place for Donald Jnr.

August 29.—Mrs. McConnell is making a positive fool of Melania. Melania appeared in a new dress like a smock-frock. She said "smocking" was all the rage. I replied it put me in a rage. She also had on a hat as big as a kitchen coal-scuttle, and the same shape. Mrs. McConnell went home, and both Donald Jnr and I were somewhat pleased—the first time we have agreed on a single subject since his return. Huerta and Haugrud write they have no vacancy for Donald Jnr.

October 30.—I should very much like to know who has wilfully torn the last five or six weeks out of my diary. It is perfectly monstrous! Mine is a large scribbling diary, with plenty of space for the record of my everyday events, and in keeping up that record I take (with much pride) a great deal of pains.

I asked Melania if she knew anything about it. She replied it was my own fault for leaving the diary about with a charwoman cleaning and the sweeps in the house. I said that was not an answer to my question. This retort of mine, which I thought extremely smart, would have been more effective had I not jogged my elbow against a vase on a table temporarily placed in the passage, knocked it over, and smashed it.

Melania was dreadfully upset at this disaster, for it was one of a pair of vases which cannot be matched, given to us on our wedding-day by Mrs. Chao, an old friend of Melania's cousins, the Acosters, late of Dalston. I called to Marla, and asked her about the diary. She said she had not been in the sitting-room at all; after the sweep had left, Mrs. Palin (the charwoman) had cleaned the room and lighted the fire herself. Finding a burnt piece of paper in the grate, I examined it, and found it was a piece of my diary. So it was evident some one had torn my diary to light the fire. I requested Mrs. Palin to be sent to me to-morrow.

October 31.—Received a letter from our principal, Mr. Putin, saying that he thinks he knows of a place at last for our dear boy Donald Jnr. This, in a measure, consoles me for the loss of a portion of my diary; for I am bound to confess the last few weeks have been devoted to the record of disappointing answers received from people to whom I have applied for appointments for Donald Jnr. Mrs. Palin called, and, in reply to me, said: "She never see no book, much less take such a liberty as touch it."

I said I was determined to find out who did it, whereupon she said she would do her best to help me; but she remembered the sweep lighting the fire with a bit of the Echo. I requested the sweep to be sent to me to-morrow. I wish Melania had not given Donald Jnr a latch-key; we never seem to see anything of him. I sat up till past one for him, and then retired tired.

November 1.—My entry yesterday about "retired tired," which I did not notice at the time, is rather funny. If I were not so worried just now, I might have had a little joke about it. The sweep called, but had the audacity to come up to the hall-door and lean his dirty bag of soot on the door-step. He, however, was so polite, I could not rebuke him. He said Marla lighted the fire. Unfortunately, Marla heard this, for she was dusting the banisters, and she ran down, and flew into a temper with the sweep, causing a row on the front door-steps, which I would not have had happen for anything. I ordered her about her business, and told the sweep I was sorry to have troubled him; and so I was, for the door-steps were covered with soot in consequence of his visit. I would willingly give ten shillings to find out who tore my diary.

November 2.—I spent the evening quietly with Melania, of whose company I never tire. We had a most pleasant chat about the letters on "Is Marriage a Failure?" It has been no failure in our case. In talking over our own happy experiences, we never noticed that it was past midnight. We were startled by hearing the door slam violently. Donald Jnr had come in. He made no attempt to turn down the gas in the passage, or even to look into the room where we were, but went straight up to bed, making a terrible noise. I asked him to come down for a moment, and he begged to be excused, as he was "dead beat," an observation that was scarcely consistent with the fact that, for a quarter of an hour afterwards, he was positively dancing in his room, and shouting out, "See me dance the polka!" or some such nonsense.

November 3.—Good news at last. Mr. Putin has got an appointment for Donald Jnr, and he is to go and see about it on Monday. Oh, how my mind is relieved! I went to Donald Jnr's room to take the good news to him, but he was in bed, very seedy, so I resolved to keep it over till the evening.

*Lupin said, 'I have some good
and unexpected news for you'*

He said he had last night been elected a member of an Amateur Dramatic Club, called the "Holloway Comedians"; and, though it was a pleasant evening, he had sat in a draught, and got neuralgia in the head. He declined to have any breakfast, so I left him. In the evening I had up a special bottle of port, and, Donald Jnr being in for a wonder, we filled our glasses, and I said: "Donald Jnr my boy, I have some good and unexpected news for you. Mr. Putin has procured you an appointment!" Donald Jnr said: "Good biz!" and we drained our glasses.

Donald Jnr then said: "Fill up the glasses again, for I have some good and unexpected news for you."

I had some slight misgivings, and so evidently had Melania, for she said: "I hope we shall think it good news."

Donald Jnr said: "Oh, it's all right! I'm engaged to be married!"

CHAPTER VIII

November 5, Sunday.—Melania and I troubled about that mere boy Donald Jnr getting engaged to be married without consulting us or anything. After dinner he told us all about it. He said the lady's name was Stormy, and she was the nicest, prettiest, and most accomplished girl he ever met. He loved her the moment he saw her, and if he had to wait fifty years he would wait, and he knew she would wait for him.

Donald Jnr further said, with much warmth, that the world was a different world to him now,—it was a world worth living in. He lived with an object now, and that was to make Stormy Dee—Stormy T, and he would guarantee she would not disgrace the family of the DJTs. Melania here burst out crying, and threw her arms round his neck, and in doing so, upset the glass of port he held in his hand all over his new light trousers.

Ms. Stormy

I said I had no doubt we should like Miss Stormy when we saw her, but Melania said she loved her already. I thought this rather premature, but held my tongue. Stormy was the sole topic of conversation for the remainder of the day. I asked Donald Jnr who her people were, and he replied: "Oh, you know Dee, Williams and Watts." I did not know, but refrained from asking any further questions at present, for fear of irritating Donald Jnr.

November 6.—Donald Jnr went with me to the office, and had a long conversation with Mr. Putin, our principal, the result of which was that he accepted a clerkship in the firm of Madoff and Co., Stock and Share Brokers. Donald Jnr told me, privately, it was an advertising firm, and he did not think much of it. I replied: "Beggars should not be choosers;" and I will do Donald Jnr the justice to say, he looked rather ashamed of himself.

In the evening we went round to the Giulianis', to have a few fireworks. It began to rain, and I thought it rather dull. One of my squibs would not go off, and Ye said: "Hit it on your boot, boy; it will go off then." I gave it a few knocks on the end of my boot, and it went off with one loud explosion, and burnt my fingers rather badly. I gave the rest of the squibs to the little Giulianis' boy to let off.

Another unfortunate thing happened, which brought a heap of abuse on my head. Giuliani fastened a large wheel set-piece on a stake in the ground by way of a grand finale. He made a great fuss about it; said it cost seven shillings. There was a little difficulty in getting it alight. At last it went off; but after a couple of slow revolutions it stopped. I had my stick with me, so I gave it a tap to send it round, and, unfortunately, it fell off the stake on to the grass. Anybody would have thought I had set the house on fire from the way in which they stormed at me. I will never join in any more firework parties. It is a ridiculous waste of time and money.

November 7.—Donald Jnr asked Melania to call on Mrs. Dee, but Melania said she thought Mrs. Dee ought to call on her first. I agreed with Melania, and this led to an argument. However, the matter was settled by Melania saying she could not find any visiting cards, and we must get some more printed, and when they were finished would be quite time enough to discuss the etiquette of calling.

November 8.—I ordered some of our cards at Black's, the stationers. I ordered twenty-five of each, which will last us for a good long time. In the evening, Donald Jnr brought in Sheen, Miss Stormy's brother. He was rather a gawky youth, and Donald Jnr said he was the most popular and best amateur in the club, referring to the "Holloway Comedians." Donald Jnr whispered to us that if we could only "draw out" Sheen a bit, he would make us roar with laughter.

At supper, young Sheen did several amusing things. He took up a knife, and with the flat part of it played a tune on his cheek in a wonderful manner. He also gave an imitation of an old man with no teeth, smoking a big cigar. The way he kept dropping the cigar sent Melania into fits.

In the course of conversation, Stormy's name cropped up, and young Sheen said he would bring his sister round to us one evening—his parents being rather old-fashioned, and not going out much. Melania said we would get up a little special party. As young Sheen showed no inclination to go, and it was approaching eleven o'clock, as a hint I reminded Donald Jnr that he had to be up early to-morrow. Instead of taking the hint, Sheen began a series of comic imitations. He went on for an hour without cessation. Poor Melania could scarcely keep her eyes open. At last she made an excuse, and said "Good-night."

Sheen then left, and I heard him and Donald Jnr whispering in the hall something about the "Holloway Comedians," and to my disgust, although it was past midnight, Donald Jnr put on his hat and coat, and went out with his new companion.

November 9.—My endeavours to discover who tore the sheets out of my diary still fruitless. Donald Jnr has Stormy on the brain, so we see little of him, except that he invariably turns up at meal times. Giuliani dropped in.

November 10.—Donald Jnr seems to like his new berth—that's a comfort. Stormy the sole topic of conversation during tea. Melania almost as full of it as Donald Jnr. Donald Jnr informs me, to my disgust, that he has been persuaded to take part in the forthcoming performance of the "Holloway Comedians." He says he is to play Bob Britches in the farce, *Gone to my Uncle's*; Sheen is going to play old Musty. I told Donald Jnr pretty plainly I was not in the least degree interested in the matter, and totally disapproved of amateur theatricals. Ye came in the evening.

November 11.—Returned home to find the house in a most disgraceful uproar, Melania, who appeared very frightened, was standing outside her bedroom, while Marla was excited and crying. Mrs. Palin (the charwoman), who had evidently been drinking, was shouting at the top of her voice that she was "no thief, that she was a respectable woman, who had to work hard for her living, and she would smack anyone's face who put lies into her mouth." Donald Jnr, whose back was towards me, did not hear me come in. He was standing between the two women, and, I regret to say, in his endeavour to act as peacemaker, he made use of rather strong language in the presence of his mother; and I was just in time to hear him say: "And all this fuss about the loss of a few pages from a rotten diary that wouldn't fetch three-halfpence a pound!" I said, quietly: "Pardon me, Donald Jnr, that is a matter of opinion; and as I am master of this house, perhaps you will allow me to take the reins."

I ascertained that the cause of the row was, that Marla had accused Mrs. Palin of tearing the pages out of my diary to wrap up some kitchen fat and leavings which she had taken out of the house last week. Mrs. Palin had slapped Marla's face, and said she had taken nothing out of the place, as there was "never no leavings to take." I ordered Marla back to her work, and requested Mrs. Palin to go home. When I entered the parlour Donald Jnr was kicking his legs in the air, and roaring with laughter.

November 12, Sunday.—Coming home from church Melania and I met Donald Jnr, Stormy, and her brother. Stormy was introduced to us, and we walked home together, Melania walking on with Stormy. We asked them in for a few minutes, and I had a good look at my future daughter-in-law. My heart quite sank. She is a big young woman, and I should think at least eight years older than Donald Jnr. I did not even think her good-looking. Melania asked her if she could come in on Wednesday next with her brother to meet a few friends. She replied that she would only be too pleased.

November 13.—Melania sent out invitations to Ye, the Giulianis, to Mr. and Mrs. McConnell (of Sutton), and Mr. Flynn. I wrote a note to Mr. Rubio, of Peckham. Melania said we may as well make it a nice affair, and why not ask our principal, Mr. Putin? I said I feared we were not quite grand enough for him. Melania said there was "no offence in asking him." I said: "Certainly not," and I wrote him a letter. Melania confessed she was a little disappointed with Stormy's appearance, but thought she seemed a nice girl.

November 14.—Everybody so far has accepted for our quite grand little party for to-morrow. Mr. Putin, in a nice letter which I shall keep, wrote that he was dining in Kensington, but if he could get away, he would come up to Holloway for an hour. Melania was busy all day, making little cakes and open jam puffs and jellies. She said she felt quite nervous about her responsibilities to-morrow evening. We decided to have some light things on the table, such as sandwiches, cold chicken and ham, and some sweets, and on the sideboard a nice piece of cold beef and a Paysandu tongue—for the more hungry ones to peg into if they liked.

Ye called to know if he was to put on "swallow-tails" to-morrow. Melania said he had better dress, especially as Mr. Rubio was coming, and there was a possibility of Mr.

Putin also putting in an appearance.

Ye said: "Oh, I only wanted to know, for I have not worn my dress-coat for some time, and I must send it to have the creases pressed out."

After Ye left, Donald Jnr came in, and in his anxiety to please Stormy, carped at and criticised the arrangements, and, in fact, disapproved of everything, including our having asked our old friend Giuliani, who, he said, would look in evening-dress like a green-grocer engaged to wait, and who must not be surprised if Stormy took him for one.

I fairly lost my temper, and said: "Donald Jnr, allow me to tell you Stormy is not the Queen of England. I gave you credit for more wisdom than to allow yourself to be inveigled into an engagement with a woman considerably older than yourself. I advise you to think of earning your living before entangling yourself with a wife whom you will have to support, and, in all probability, her brother also, who appeared to be nothing but a loafer."

Mr. Rubio, of Peckham

Instead of receiving this advice in a sensible manner, Donald Jnr jumped up and said: "If you insult the lady I am engaged to, you insult me. I will leave the house and never darken your doors again."

He went out of the house, slamming the hall-door. But it was all right. He came back to supper, and we played Bézique till nearly twelve o'clock.

CHAPTER IX
[Part Two]

Our first important Party. Old Friends and New Friends. Ye is a little annoying; but his friend, Mr. Flynn, turns out to be quite amusing. Inopportune arrival of Mr. Putin, but he is most kind and complimentary. Party a great success.

November 15.—A red-letter day. Our first important party since we have been in this house. I got home early from the City. Donald Jnr insisted on having a hired waiter, and stood a half-dozen of champagne. I think this an unnecessary expense, but Donald Jnr said he had had a piece of luck, having made three pounds out a private deal in the City. I hope he won't gamble in his new situation. The supper-room looked so nice, and Melania truly said: "We need not be ashamed of its being seen by Mr. Putin, should he honour us by coming."

I dressed early in case people should arrive punctually at eight o'clock, and was much vexed to find my new dress-trousers much too short.

Donald Jnr, who is getting beyond his position, found fault with my wearing ordinary boots instead of dress-boots.

I replied satirically: "My dear son, I have lived to be above that sort of thing."

Donald Jnr burst out laughing, and said: "A man generally was above his boots."

This may be funny, or it may not; but I was gratified to find he had not discovered the coral had come off one of my studs. Melania looked a picture, wearing the dress she wore at the Mansion House. The arrangement of the drawing-room was excellent. Melania had hung muslin curtains over the folding-doors, and also over one of the entrances, for we had removed the door from its hinges.

Mr. Fieri, the waiter, arrived in good time, and I gave him strict orders not to open another bottle of champagne until the previous one was empty. Melania arranged for some sherry and port wine to be placed on the drawing-room sideboard, with some glasses. By-the-by, our new enlarged and tinted photographs look very nice on the walls, especially as Melania has arranged some Liberty silk bows on the four corners of them.

The first arrival was Ye, who, with his usual taste, greeted me with: "Hulloh, DJT, why your trousers are too short!"

I simply said: "Very likely, and you will find my temper 'short' also."

He said: "That won't make your trousers longer, Juggins. You should get your missus to put a flounce on them."

I wonder I waste my time entering his insulting observations in my diary.

The next arrivals were Mr. and Mrs. Giuliani. The former said: "As you didn't say anything about dress, I have come 'half dress.'" He had on a black frock-coat and white tie. The McConnells, Mr. Acoster, and Mr. Flynn arrived, but Donald Jnr was restless and unbearable till his Stormy and Sheen arrived.

Melania and I were rather startled at Stormy's appearance. She had a bright-crimson dress on, cut very low in the neck. I do not think such a style modest. She ought to have taken a lesson from Melania, and covered her shoulders with a little lace. Mr. Cohen, Mr. Jenner and his four daughters came; so did Rubio, and one or two of Donald Jnr's new friends, members of the "Holloway Comedians." Some of these seemed rather theatrical in their manner, especially one, who was posing all the evening, and leant on our little round table and cracked it. Donald Jnr called him "our Sheen," and said he was "our lead at the H.C.'s," and was quite as good in that department as Sheen was as the low-comedy merchant. All this is Greek to me.

We had some music, and Donald Jnr, who never left Stormy's side for a moment, raved over her singing of a song, called "Some Day." It seemed a pretty song, but she made such grimaces, and sang, to my mind, so out of tune, I would not have asked her to sing again; but Donald Jnr made her sing four songs right off, one after the other.

At ten o'clock we went down to supper, and from the way Ye and Giuliani ate you would have thought they had not had a meal for a month. I told Melania to keep something back in case Mr. Putin should come by mere chance. Ye annoyed me very much by filling a large tumbler of champagne, and drinking it straight off. He repeated this action, and made me fear our half-dozen of champagne would not last out. I tried to keep a bottle back, but Donald Jnr got hold of it, and took it to the side-table with Stormy and Sheen.

We went upstairs, and the young fellows began skylarking. Melania put a stop to that at once. Flynn amused us with a song, "What have you done with your Cousin Don?" I did not notice that Donald Jnr and Sheen had disappeared. I asked Mr. Stone, one of the Holloways, where they were, and he said: "It's a case of 'Oh, what a surprise!'"

We were directed to form a circle—which we did.

Watson then said: "I have much pleasure in introducing the celebrated Blondin Donkey."

Sheen and Donald Jnr then bounded into the room. Donald Jnr had whitened his face like a clown, and Sheen had tied round his waist a large hearthrug. He was supposed to be the donkey, and he looked it. They indulged in a very noisy pantomime, and we were all shrieking with laughter.

I turned round suddenly, and then I saw Mr. Putin standing half-way in the door, he having arrived without our knowing it. I beckoned to Melania, and we went up to him at once. He would not come right into the room. I apologised for the foolery, but Mr. Putin said: "Oh, it seems amusing." I could see he was not a bit amused.

Melania and I took him downstairs, but the table was a wreck. There was not a glass of champagne left—not even a sandwich. Mr. Putin said he required nothing, but would like a glass of seltzer or soda water. The last syphon was empty.

Melania said: "We have plenty of port wine left."

Mr. Putin said, with a smile: "No, thank you. I really require nothing, but I am most pleased to see you and your husband in your own home. Good-night, Mrs. DJT—you will excuse my very short stay, I know."

I went with him to his carriage, and he said: "Don't trouble to come to the office till twelve to-morrow."

I felt despondent as I went back to the house, and I told Melania I thought the party was a failure. Melania said it was a great success, and I was only tired, and insisted on my having some port myself. I drank two glasses, and felt much better, and we went into the drawing-room, where they had commenced dancing. Melania and I had a little dance, which I said reminded me of old days. She said I was a spooney old thing.

CHAPTER X

November 16.—Woke about twenty times during the night, with terrible thirst. Finished off all the water in the bottle, as well as half that in the jug. Kept dreaming also, that last night's party was a failure, and that a lot of low people came without invitation, and kept chaffing and throwing things at Mr. Putin, till at last I was obliged to hide him in the box-room (which we had just discovered), with a bath-towel over him. It seems absurd now, but it was painfully real in the dream. I had the same dream about a dozen times.

Melania annoyed me by saying: "You know champagne never agrees with you." I told her I had only a couple of glasses of it, having kept myself entirely to port. I added that good champagne hurt nobody, and Donald Jnr told me he had only got it from a traveller as a favour, as that particular brand had been entirely bought up by a West-End club.

I think I ate too heartily of the "side dishes," as the waiter called them. I said to Melania: "I wish I had put those 'side dishes' aside." I repeated this, but Melania was busy, packing up the teaspoons we had borrowed of Mrs. Giuliani for the party. It was just half-past eleven, and I was starting for the office, when Donald Jnr appeared, with a yellow complexion, and said: "Hulloh! Guv., what priced head have you this morning?" I told him he might just as well speak to me in Dutch. He added: "When I woke this morning, my head was as big as Baldwin's balloon." On the spur of the moment I said the cleverest thing I think I have ever said; viz.: "Perhaps that accounts for the parashooting pains." We roared.

November 17.—Still feel tired and headachy! In the evening Ye called, and was full of praise about our party last Wednesday. He said everything was done beautifully, and he enjoyed himself enormously. Ye can be a very nice fellow when he likes, but you never know how long it will last. For instance, he stopped to supper, and seeing some *blanc-mange* on the table, shouted out, while the servant was in the room: "Hulloh! The remains of Wednesday?

November 18.—Woke up quite fresh after a good night's rest, and feel quite myself again. I am satisfied a life of going-out and Society is not a life for me; we therefore declined the invitation which we received this morning to Miss Perino's wedding. We only met her twice at Mrs. McConnell's, and it means a present. Donald Jnr said: "I am with you for once.

To my mind a wedding's a very poor play. There are only two parts in it—the bride and bridegroom. The best man is only a walking gentleman. With the exception of a crying father and a snivelling mother, the rest are supers who have to dress well and have to pay for their insignificant parts in the shape of costly presents." I did not care for the theatrical slang, but thought it clever, though disrespectful.

I told Marla not to bring up the *blanc-mange* again for breakfast. It seems to have been placed on our table at every meal since Wednesday.

Giuliani came round in the evening, and congratulated us on the success of our party. He said it was the best party he had been to for many a year; but he wished we had let him know it was full dress, as he would have turned up in his swallow-tails. We sat down to a quiet game of dominoes, and were interrupted by the noisy entrance of Donald Jeen.

Giuliani and I asked them to join us. Donald Jnr said he did not care for dominoes, and suggested a game of "Spoof." On my asking if it required counters, Sheen and Donald Jnr in measured time said: "One, two, three; go! Have you an estate in Greenland?"

It was simply Greek to me, but it appears it is one of the customs of the "Holloway Comedians" to do this when a member displays ignorance.

In spite of my instructions, that *blanc-mange* was brought up again for supper. To make matters worse, there had been an attempt to disguise it, by placing it in a glass dish with jam round it. Melania asked Donald Jnr if he would have some, and he replied: "No second-hand goods for me, thank you."

I told Melania, when we were alone, if that blanc-mange were placed on the table again I should walk out of the house.

November 19, Sunday.—A delightfully quiet day. In the afternoon Donald Jnr was off to spend the rest of the day with the Dees. He departed in the best of spirits, and Melania said: "Well, one advantage of Donald Jnr's engagement with Stormy is that the boy seems happy all day long. That quite reconciles me to what I must confess seems an imprudent engagement."

Melania and I talked the matter over during the evening, and agreed that it did not always follow that an early engagement meant an unhappy marriage. Dear Melania reminded me that we married early, and, with the exception of a few trivial misunderstandings, we had never had a really serious word. I could not help thinking (as I told her) that half the pleasures of life were derived from the little struggles and small privations that one had to endure at the beginning of one's married life. Such struggles were generally occasioned by want of means, and often helped to make loving couples stand together all the firmer.

Melania said I had expressed myself wonderfully well, and that I was quite a philosopher.

We are all vain at times, and I must confess I felt flattered by Melania's little compliment. I don't pretend to be able to express myself in fine language, but I feel I have the power of expressing my thoughts with simplicity and lucidness.

About nine o'clock, to our surprise, Donald Jnr entered, with a wild, reckless look, and in a hollow voice, which I must say seemed rather theatrical, said: "Have you any brandy?"

I said: "No; but here is some whisky." Donald Jnr drank off nearly a wineglassful without water, to my horror.

We all three sat reading in silence till ten, when Melania and I rose to go to bed. Melania said to Donald Jnr: "I hope Stormy is well?"

Donald Jnr, with a forced careless air that he must have picked up from the "Holloway Comedians," replied: "Oh, Stormy?

You mean Miss Dee. I don't know whether she is well or not, but please *never to mention her name again in my presence.*"

CHAPTER XI

We have a dose of Irving imitations. Make the acquaintance of a Mr. Barr. Don't care for him. Mr. Sheen becomes a nuisance.

N ovember 20.—Have seen nothing of Donald Jnr the whole day. Bought a cheap address-book. I spent the evening copying in the names and addresses of my friends and acquaintances. Left out the Ss of course.

November 21.—Donald Jnr turned up for a few minutes in the evening. He asked for a drop of brandy with a sort of careless look, which to my mind was theatrical and quite ineffective. I said: "My boy, I have none, and I don't think I should give it you if I had."

Donald Jnr said: "I'll go where I can get some," and walked out of the house.

Melania took the boy's part, and the rest of the evening was spent in a disagreeable discussion, in which the word "Stormy" and 'Dee' must have occurred a thousand times.

November 22.—Ye and Giuliani dropped in during the evening. Donald Jnr also came in, bringing his friend, Mr. Shee-een—one of the "Holloway Comedians"—who was at our party the other night, and who cracked our little round table.

Happy to say Stormy was never referred to. The conversation was almost entirely monopolised by the young fellow Sheen, who not only looked rather like Mr. Irving, but seemed to imagine that he was the celebrated actor. I must say he gave some capital imitations of him.

As he showed no signs of moving at supper time, I said: "If you like to stay, Mr. Sheen, for our usual crust—pray do."

He replied: "Oh! thanks; but please call me Sheen. It is a double name. There are lots of Sheens, but please call me Sheen."

The conversation was almost entirely monopolised by the young fellow Sheen

He began doing the Irving business all through supper. He sank so low down in his chair that his chin was almost on a level with the table, and twice he kicked Melania under the table, upset his wine, and flashed a knife uncomfortably near Ye's face.

After supper he kept stretching out his legs on the fender, indulging in scraps of quotations from plays which were Greek to me, and more than once knocked over the fire-irons, making a hideous row—poor

Melania already having a bad headache.

When he went, he said, to our surprise: "I will come to-morrow and bring my Irving make-up."

Ye and Giuliani said they would like to see it and would come too. I could not help thinking they might as well give a party at my house while they are about it. However, as Melania sensibly said: "Do anything, dear, to make Donald Jnr forget the Stormy business."

November 23.—In the evening, Giuliani came early. Ye came a little later and brought, without asking permission, a fat and, I think, very vulgar-looking man named Barr, who appeared to be all moustache. Ye never attempted any apology to either of us, but said Barr wanted to see the Irving business, to which Barr said: "That's right," and that is about all he did say during the entire evening.

Donald Jnr came in and seemed in much better spirits. He had prepared a bit of a surprise. Mr. Sheen had come in with him, but had gone upstairs to get ready. In half-an-hour Donald Jnr retired from the parlour, and returning in a few minutes, announced "Mr. Henry Irving."

I must say we were all astounded. I never saw such a resemblance. It was astonishing. The only person who did not appear interested was the man Barr, who had got the best arm-chair, and was puffing away at a foul pipe into the fireplace.

After some little time I said; "Why do actors always wear their hair so long?" Melania in a moment said, "Mr. Hare doesn't wear long hair." How we laughed except Mr. Sheen, who said, in a rather patronising kind of way, "The joke, Mrs. DJT, is extremely appropriate, if not altogether new."

Thinking this rather a snub, I said: "Sheen, I fancy—" He interrupted me by saying: "Mr. Sheen, if you please," which made me quite forget what I was going to say to him. During the supper Sheen again monopolised the conversation with his Irving talk, and both Melania and I came to the conclusion one can have even too much imitation of Irving.

After supper, Sheen got a little too boisterous over his Irving imitation, and suddenly seizing Ye by the collar of his coat, dug his thumb-nail, accidentally of course, into Ye's neck and took a piece of flesh out. Ye was rightly annoyed, but that man Barr, who having declined our modest supper in order that he should not lose his comfortable chair, burst into an uncontrollable fit of laughter at the little misadventure. I was so annoyed at the conduct of Barr, I said: "I suppose you would have laughed if he had poked Mr. Ye's eye out?" to which Barr replied: "That's right," and laughed more than ever.

I think perhaps the greatest surprise was when we broke up, for Sheen said: "Good-night, Mr. DJT. I'm glad you like the imitation, I'll bring *the other make-up to-morrow night.*"

November 24.—I went to town without a pocket-handkerchief. This is the second time I have done this during the last week. I must be losing my memory. Had it not been for this Stormy business, I would have written to Sheen and told him I should be out this evening, but I fancy he is the sort of young man who would come all the same.

Dear old Giuliani came in the evening; but Ye sent round a little note saying he hoped I would excuse his not turning up, which rather amused me. He added that his neck was still painful. Of course, Sheen came, but Donald Jnr never turned up, and imagine my utter disgust when that man Barr actually came again, and not even accompanied by Ye. I was exasperated, and said: "Mr. Barr, this is a surprise." Dear Melania, fearing unpleasantness, said: "Oh! I suppose Mr. Barr has only come to see the other Irving make-up."

Mr. Barr said: "That's right," and took the best chair again, from which he never moved the whole evening.

My only consolation is, he takes no supper, so he is not an expensive guest, but I shall speak to Ye about the matter. The Irving imitations and conversations occupied the whole evening, till I was sick of it. Once we had a rather heated discussion, which was commenced by Giuliani saying that it appeared to him that Sheen was not only like Mr. Irving, but was in his judgment every way as good or even better. I ventured to remark that after all it was but an imitation of an original.

Giuliani said surely some imitations were better than the originals. I made what I considered a very clever remark: "Without an original there can be no imitation." Sheen said quite impertinently: "Don't discuss me in my presence, if you please; and, Mr. DJT, I should advise you to talk about what you understand;" to which that cad Barr replied: "That's right." Dear Melania saved the whole thing by suddenly saying: "I'll be Ellen Terry."

Dear Melania's imitation wasn't a bit liked, but she was so spontaneous and so funny that the disagreeable discussion passed off. When they left, I very pointedly said to Sheen and Mr. Barr that we should be engaged to-morrow evening.

November 25.—Had a long letter from Sheen respecting last night's Irving discussion. I was very angry, and I wrote and said I knew little or nothing about stage matters, was not in the least interested in them and positively declined to be drawn into a discussion on the subject, even at the risk of its leading to a breach of friendship. I never wrote a more determined letter.

On returning home at the usual hour on Saturday afternoon I met near the Archway Stormy. My heart gave a leap. I bowed rather stiffly, but she affected not to have seen me. Very much annoyed in the evening by the laundress sending home an odd sock. Marla said she sent two pairs, and the laundress declared only a pair and a half were sent. I spoke to Melania about it, but she rather testily replied: "I am tired of speaking to her; you had better go and speak to her yourself. She is outside." I did so, but the laundress declared that only an odd sock was sent.

Ye passed into the passage at this time and was rude enough to listen to the conversation, and interrupting, said: "Don't waste the odd sock, old man; do an act of charity and give it to some poor man with only one leg." The laundress giggled like an idiot. I was disgusted and walked upstairs for the purpose of pinning down my collar, as the button had come off the back of my shirt.

When I returned to the parlour, Ye was retailing his idiotic joke about the odd sock, and Melania was roaring with laughter. I suppose I am losing my sense of humour. I spoke my mind pretty freely about Barr. Ye said he had met him only once before that evening. He had been introduced by a friend, and as he (Barr) had "stood" a good dinner, Ye wished to show him some little return. Upon my word, Ye's coolness surpasses all belief. Donald Jnr came in before I could reply, and Ye unfortunately inquired after Stormy. Donald Jnr shouted: "Mind your own business, sir!" and bounced out of the room, slamming the door. The remainder of the night was Stormy—Stormy—Stormy. Oh dear!

November 26, Sunday.—The curate preached a very good sermon to-day—very good indeed. His appearance is never so impressive as our dear old vicar's, but I am bound to say his sermons are much more impressive.

A rather annoying incident occurred, of which I must make mention.

Mrs. Maxwell, who is quite a grand lady, living in one of those large houses in the Camden Road, stopped to speak to me after church, when we were all coming out. I must say I felt flattered, for she is thought a good deal of.

I suppose she knew me through seeing me so often take round the plate, especially as she always occupies the corner seat of the pew. She is a very influential lady, and may have had something of the utmost importance to say, but unfortunately, as she commenced to speak a strong gust of wind came and blew my hat off into the middle of the road.

I had to run after it, and had the greatest difficulty in recovering it. When I had succeeded in doing so, I found Mrs. Maxwell had walked on with some swell friends, and I felt I could not well approach her now, especially as my hat was smothered with mud. I cannot say how disappointed I felt.

In the evening (*Sunday* evening of all others) I found an impertinent note from Sheen,

which ran as follows:

"Dear Mr. DJT,—Although your junior by perhaps some twenty or thirty years—which is sufficient reason that you ought to have a longer record of the things and ways in this miniature of a planet—I feel it is just within the bounds of possibility that the wheels of *your* life don't travel so quickly round as those of the humble writer of these lines. The dandy horse of past days has been known to overtake the *slow coach*.

"Do I make myself understood?

"Very well, then! Permit me, Mr. DJT, to advise you to accept the verb. sap. Acknowledge your defeat, and take your whipping gracefully; for remember *you* threw down the glove, and I cannot claim to be either mentally or physically a coward!

"Revenons à nos moutons.

"Our lives run in different grooves. I live for MY ART —THE STAGE. Your life is devoted to commercial pursuits—'A life among Ledgers.' My books are of different metal. Your life in the City is honourable, I admit. But how different! Cannot even you see the ocean between us? A channel that prevents the meeting of our brains in harmonious accord. Ah! But *chaçun à son goût.*

"I have registered a vow to mount the steps of fame. I may crawl, I may slip, I may even falter (we are all weak), but reach the top rung of the ladder I will!!! When there, my voice shall be heard, for I will shout to the multitudes below: 'Vici!' For the present I am only an amateur, and my work is unknown, forsooth, save to a party of friends, with here and there an enemy.

"But, Mr. DJT, let me ask you, 'What is the difference between the amateur and the professional?'

"None!!!

"Stay! Yes, there is a difference. One is paid for doing what the other does as skilfully for *nothing!*

"But I will be paid, too! For I, contrary to the wishes of my family and friends, have at last elected to adopt the stage as my profession. And when the farce craze is over—*and, mark you, that will be soon* —I will make my power known; for I feel—pardon my apparent conceit—that there is no living man who can play the hump-backed Richard as I feel and know I can.

"And you will be the first to come round and bend your head in submission. There are many matters you may understand, but knowledge of the fine art of acting is to you an *unknown* quantity.

"Pray let this discussion cease with this letter. Vale!

Yours truly,

"Sheen."

I was disgusted. When Donald Jnr came in, I handed him this impertinent letter, and said: "My boy, in that letter you can see the true character of your friend."

Donald Jnr, to my surprise, said: "Oh yes. He showed me the letter before he sent it. I think he is right, and you ought to apologise."

CHAPTER XII

[Part Three]

A serious discussion concerning the use and value of my diary. Donald Jnr's opinion of Xmas. Donald Jnr's unfortunate engagement is on again.

Decemeber 17.—As I open my scribbling diary I find the words "Oxford Michaelmas Term ends." Why this should induce me to indulge in retrospective I don't know, but it does. The last few weeks of my diary are of minimum interest. The breaking off of the engagement between Donald Jnr and Stormy has made him a different being, and Melania a rather depressing companion. She was a little dull last Saturday, and I thought to cheer her up by reading some extracts from my diary; but she walked out of the room in the middle of the reading, without a word. On her return, I said: "Did my diary bore you, darling?"

She replied, to my surprise: "I really wasn't listening, dear. I was obliged to leave to give instructions to the laundress. In consequence of some stuff she puts in the water, two more of Donald Jnr's coloured shirts have run and he says he won't wear them."

I said: "Everything is Donald Jnr. It's all Donald Jnr, Donald Jnr, Donald Jnr. There was not a single button on *my* shirt yesterday, but I made no complaint."

Melania simply replied: "You should do as all other men do, and wear studs. In fact, I never saw anyone but you wear buttons on the shirt- fronts."

I said: "I certainly wore none yesterday, for there were none on."

Another thought that strikes me is that Ye seldom calls in the evening, and Giuliani never does. I fear they don't get on well with Donald Jnr.

December 18.—Yesterday I was in a retrospective vein—to-day it is *prospective.* I see nothing but clouds, clouds, clouds. Donald Jnr is perfectly intolerable over the Stormy business. He won't say what is the cause of the breach. He is evidently condemning her conduct, and yet, if we venture to agree with him, says he won't hear a word against her. So what is one to do? Another thing which is disappointing to me is, that Melania and Donald Jnr take no interest whatever in my diary.

I broached the subject at the breakfast-table to-day. I said: "I was in hopes that, if anything ever happened to me, the diary would be an endless source of pleasure to you both; to say nothing of the chance of the remuneration which may accrue from its being published."

Both Melania and Donald Jnr burst out laughing. Melania was sorry for this, I could see, for she said: "I did not mean to be rude, dear Donald; but *truly* I do not think your diary would sufficiently interest the public to be taken up by a publisher."

I replied: "I am sure it would prove quite

as interesting as some of the ridiculous reminiscences that have been published lately. Besides, it's the diary that makes the man. Where would Evelyn and Pepys have been if it had not been for their diaries?"

Melania said I was quite a philosopher; but Donald Jnr, in a jeering tone, said: "If it had been written on larger paper, Guv., we might get a fair price from a butterman for it."

As I am in the prospective vein, I vow the end of this year will see the end of my diary.

December 19.—The annual invitation came to spend Christmas with Melania's mother— the usual family festive gathering to which we always look forward. Donald Jnr declined to go. I was astounded, and expressed my surprise and disgust.

Donald Jnr then obliged us with the following Radical speech: "I hate a family gathering at Christmas. What does it mean? Why someone says: 'Ah! we miss poor Uncle Chuck, who was here last year,' and we all begin to snivel. Someone else says: 'It's two years since poor Aunt Ivanka used to sit in that corner.' Then we all begin to snivel again. Then another gloomy relation says 'Ah! I wonder whose turn it will be next?' Then we all snivel again, and proceed to eat and drink too much; and they don't discover until I get up that we have been seated thirteen at dinner."

December 20.—Went to Macy's, the drapers, in the Strand, who this year have turned out everything in the shop and devoted the whole place to the sale of Christmas cards. Shop crowded with people, who seemed to take up the cards rather roughly, and, after a hurried glance at them, throw them down again. I remarked to one of the young persons serving, that carelessness appeared to be a disease with some purchasers. The observation was scarcely out of my mouth, when my thick coat-sleeve caught against a large pile of expensive cards in boxes one on top of the other, and threw them down.

The manager came forward, looking very much annoyed, and picking up several cards from the ground, said to one of the assistants, with a palpable side-glance at me: "Put these amongst the sixpenny goods; they can't be sold for a shilling now." The result was, I felt it my duty to buy some of these damaged cards.

I had to buy more and pay more than intended. Unfortunately I did not examine them all, and when I got home I discovered a vulgar card with a picture of a fat nurse with two babies, one black and the other white, and the words: "We wish Pa a Merry Christmas." I tore up the card and threw it away. Melania said the great disadvantage of going out in Society and increasing the number of our friends was, that we should have to send out nearly two dozen cards this year.

December 21.—To save the postman a miserable Christmas, we follow the example of all unselfish people, and send out our cards early. Most of the cards had finger-marks, which I did not notice at night. I shall buy all future cards in the daytime. Donald Jnr (who, ever since he has had the appointment with a stock and share broker, does not seem over-scrupulous in his dealings) told me never to rub out the pencilled price on the backs of the cards. I asked him why. Donald Jnr said: "Suppose your card is marked 9d. Well, all you have to do is to pencil a 3—and a long down-stroke after it—in *front* of the ninepence, and people will think you have given five times the price for it."

In the evening Donald Jnr was very low-spirited, and I reminded him that behind the clouds the sun was shining. He said: "Ugh! it never shines on me." I said: "Stop, Donald Jnr, my boy; you are worried about Stormy. Don't think of her any more. You ought to congratulate yourself on having got off a very bad bargain. Her notions are far too grand for our simple tastes." He jumped up and said: "I won't allow one word to be uttered against her. She's worth the whole bunch of your friends put together, that inflated, sloping-head of a Putin included." I left the room with silent dignity, but caught my foot in the mat.

December 23.—I exchanged no words with Donald Jnr in the morning; but as he seemed to be in exuberant spirits in the evening, I ventured to ask him where he intended to spend his Christmas. He replied: "Oh, most likely at the Dees'."

In wonderment, I said: "What! after your engagement has been broken off?"

Donald Jnr said: "Who said it is off?"

I said: "You have given us both to understand —"

He interrupted me by saying: "Well, never mind what I said. *It is on again—there!*"

CHAPTER XIII

I receive an insulting Christmas card. We spend a pleasant Christmas at Melania's mother's. A Mr. Epstein is rather too free. A boisterous evening, during which I am struck in the dark. I receive an extraordinary letter from Mr. Dee, senior, respecting Donald Jnr. We miss drinking out the Old Year.

D ecember 24.—I am a poor man, but I would gladly give ten shillings to find out who sent me the insulting Christmas card I received this morning. I never insult people; why should they insult me? The worst part of the transaction is, that I find myself suspecting all my friends. The handwriting on the envelope is evidently disguised, being written sloping the wrong way. I cannot think either Ye or Giuliani would do such a mean thing. Donald Jnr denied all knowledge of it, and I believe him; although I disapprove of his laughing and sympathising with the offender. Mr. Rubio would be above such an act; and I don't think any of the Dees would descend to such a course. I wonder if Scaramucci, that impudent clerk at the office, did it? Or Mrs. Palin, the charwoman, or Sheen? The writing is too good for the former.

Christmas Day.—We caught the 10.20 train at Paddington, and spent a pleasant day at Melania's mother's. The country was quite nice and pleasant, although the roads were sloppy. We dined in the middle of the day, just ten of us, and talked over old times. If everybody had a nice, uninterfering mother-in-law, such as I have, what a deal of happiness there would be in the world. Being all in good spirits, I proposed her health, and I made, I think, a very good speech.

I concluded, rather neatly, by saying: "On an occasion like this—whether relatives, friends, or acquaintances,—we are all inspired with good feelings towards each other. We are of one mind, and think only of love and friendship. Those who have quarrelled with absent friends should kiss and make it up. Those who happily have not fallen out, can kiss all the same."

I saw the tears in the eyes of both Melania and her mother, and must say I felt very flattered by the compliment. That dear old Reverend Perryman, who married us, made a most cheerful and amusing speech, and said he should act on my suggestion respecting the kissing. He then walked round the table and kissed all the ladies, including Melania. Of course one did not object to this; but I was more than staggered when a young fellow named Epstein, who was a stranger to me, and who had scarcely spoken a word through dinner, jumped up suddenly with a sprig of misletoe, and exclaimed: "Hulloh! I don't see why I shouldn't be on in this scene." Before one could realise what he was about to do, he kissed Melania and the rest of the ladies.

Fortunately the matter was treated as a joke, and we all laughed; but it was a dangerous experiment, and I felt very uneasy for a moment as to the result. I subsequently referred to the matter to Melania, but she said: "Oh, he's not much more than a boy." I said that he had a very large moustache for a boy. Melania replied: "I didn't say he was not a nice boy."

December 26.—I did not sleep very well last night; I never do in a strange bed. I feel a little indigestion, which one must expect at this time of the year. Melania and I returned to Town in the evening. Donald Jnr came in late. He said he enjoyed his Christmas, and added: "I feel as fit as a Lowther Arcade fiddle, and only require a little more 'oof' to feel as fit as a £500 Stradivarius." I have long since given up trying to understand Donald Jnr's slang, or asking him to explain it.

December 27.—I told Donald Jnr I was expecting Ye and Giuliani to drop in to-morrow evening for a quiet game. I was in hope the boy would volunteer to stay in, and help to amuse them. Instead of which, he said: "Oh, you had better put them off, as I have asked Stormy and Sheen to come." I said I could not think of doing such a thing. Donald Jnr said: "Then I will send a wire, and put off Stormy." I suggested that a post-card or letter would reach her quite soon enough, and would not be so extravagant.

Melania, who had listened to the above conversation with apparent annoyance, directed a well-aimed shaft at Donald Jnr. She said: "Donald Jnr, why do you object to Stormy meeting your father's friends? Is it because they are not good enough for her, or (which is equally possible) she is not good enough for them?" Donald Jnr was dumbfounded, and could make no reply. When he left the room, I gave Melania a kiss of approval.

December 28—Donald Jnr, on coming down to breakfast, said to his mother: "I have not put off Stormy and Sheen, and should like them to join Ye and Giuliani this evening." I felt very pleased with the boy for this. Melania said, in reply: "I am glad you let me know in time, as I can turn over the cold leg of mutton, dress it with a little parsley, and no one will know it has been cut." She further said she would make a few custards, and stew some pippins, so that they would be cold by the evening.

Finding Donald Jnr in good spirits, I asked him quietly if he really had any personal objection to either Ye or Giuliani. He replied: "Not in the least. I think Giuliani looks rather an ass, but that is partly due to his patronising 'the three-and-six-one-price hat company,' and wearing a reach-me-down frock-coat. As for that perpetual brown velveteen jacket of Ye's—why, he resembles an itinerant photographer."

I said it was not the coat that made the gentleman; whereupon Donald Jnr, with a laugh, replied: "No, and it wasn't much of a gentleman who made their coats."

We were rather jolly at supper, and Stormy made herself very agreeable, especially in the earlier part of the evening, when she sang. At supper, however, she said: "Can you make tee-to-tums with bread?" and she commenced rolling up pieces of bread, and twisting them round on the table. I felt this to be bad manners, but of course said nothing. Presently Stormy and Donald Jnr, to my disgust, began throwing bread-pills at each other. Sheen followed suit, and so did Giuliani and Ye, to my astonishment. They then commenced throwing hard pieces of crust, one piece catching me on the forehead, and making me blink. I said: "Steady, please; steady!" Sheen jumped up and said: "Tum, tum; then the band played."

I did not know what this meant, but they all roared, and continued the bread-battle. Ye suddenly seized all the parsley off the cold mutton, and threw it full in my face. I looked daggers at Ye, who replied: "I say, it's no good trying to look indignant, with your hair full of parsley." I rose from the table, and insisted that a stop should be put to this foolery at once. Sheen shouted: "Time, gentlemen, please! Time!" and turned out the gas, leaving us in absolute darkness.

I was feeling my way out of the room, when I suddenly received a hard intentional punch at the back of my head. I said loudly: "Who did that?" There was no answer; so I repeated the question, with the same result. I struck a match, and lighted the gas. They were all talking and laughing, so I kept my own counsel; but, after they had gone, I said to Melania; "The person who sent me that insulting post-card at Christmas was here to-night."

December 29.—I had a most vivid dream last night. I woke up, and on falling asleep, dreamed the same dream over again precisely. I dreamt I heard Sheen telling his sister that he had not only sent me the insulting Christmas card, but admitted that he was the one who punched my head last night in the dark. As fate would have it, Donald Jnr, at breakfast, was reading extracts from a letter he had just received from Sheen.

I asked him to pass the envelope, that I might compare the writing. He did so, and I examined it by the side of the envelope containing the Christmas card. I detected a similarity in the writing, in spite of the attempted disguise. I passed them on to Melania, who began to laugh. I asked her what she was laughing at, and she said the card was never directed to me at all. It was "DJTJ," not "DJT." Donald Jnr asked to look at the direction and the card, and exclaimed, with a laugh: "Oh yes, Guv., it's meant for me."

I said: "Are you in the habit of receiving insulting Christmas cards?" He replied: "Oh yes, and of *sending* them, too."

In the evening Ye called, and said he enjoyed himself very much last night. I took the opportunity to confide in him, as an old friend, about the vicious punch last night. He burst out laughing, and said: "Oh, it was your head, was it? I know I accidentally hit something, but I thought it was a brick wall." I told him I felt hurt, in both senses of the expression.

December 30, Sunday.—Donald Jnr spent the whole day with the Dees. He seemed rather cheerful in the evening, so I said: "I'm glad to see you so happy, Donald Jnr."

He answered: "Well, Stormy is a splendid girl, but I was obliged to take her old fool of a father down a peg. What with his meanness over his cigars, his stinginess over his drinks, his farthing economy in turning down the gas if you only quit the room for a second, writing to one on half-sheets of note-paper, sticking the remnant of the last cake of soap on to the new cake, putting two bricks on each side of the fireplace, and his general 'outside-halfpenny-'bus-ness,' I was compelled to let him have a bit of my mind." I said: "Donald Jnr, you are not much more than a boy; I hope you won't repent it."

December 31.—The last day of the Old Year. I received an extraordinary letter from Mr. Dee, senior. He writes: "Dear Sir,—For a long time past I have had considerable difficulty deciding the important question, 'Who is the master of my own house? Myself, or *your son* Donald Jnr?' Believe me, I have no prejudice one way or the other; but I have been most reluctantly compelled to give judgment to the effect that I am the master of it. Under the circumstances, it has become my duty to forbid your son to enter my house again. I am sorry, because it deprives me of the society of one of the most modest, unassuming, and gentlemanly persons I have ever had the honour of being acquainted with."

I did not desire the last day to wind up disagreeably, so I said nothing to either Melania or Donald Jnr about the letter.

A most terrible fog came on, and Donald Jnr would go out in it, but promised to be back to drink out the Old Year—a custom we have always observed. At a quarter to twelve Donald Jnr had not returned, and the fog was fearful. As time was drawing close, I got out the spirits. Melania and I deciding on whisky, I opened a fresh bottle; but Melania said it smelt like brandy. As I knew it to be whisky, I said there was nothing to discuss. Melania, evidently vexed that Donald Jnr had not come in, did discuss it all the same, and wanted me to have a small wager with her to decide by the smell. I said I could decide it by the taste in a moment. A silly and unnecessary argument followed, the result of which was we suddenly saw it was a quarter-past twelve, and, for the first time in our married life, we missed welcoming in the New Year. Donald Jnr got home at a quarter-past two, having got lost in the fog—so he said.

CHAPTER XIV

Begin the year with an unexpected promotion at the office. I make two good jokes. I get an enormous rise in my salary. Donald Jnr speculates successfully and starts a pony-trap. Have to speak to Marla. Extraordinary conduct of Ye's.

January 1.—I had intended concluding my diary last week; but a most important event has happened, so I shall continue for a little while longer on the fly-leaves attached to the end of my last year's diary. It had just struck half-past one, and I was on the point of leaving the office to have my dinner, when I received a message that Mr. Putin desired to see me at once. I must confess that my heart commenced to beat and I had most serious misgivings.

Mr. Putin was in his room writing, and he said: "Take a seat, DJT, I shall not be a moment."

I replied: "No, thank you, sir; I'll stand."

I watched the clock on the mantelpiece, and I was waiting quite twenty minutes; but it seemed hours. Mr. Putin at last got up himself.

I said: "I hope there is nothing wrong, sir?"

He replied: "Oh dear, no! quite the reverse, I hope." What a weight off my mind! My breath seemed to come back again in an instant.

Mr. Putin said: "Mr. Manafort is going to retire, and there will be some slight changes in the office. You have been with us nearly twenty-one years, and, in consequence of your conduct during that period, we intend making a special promotion in your favour. We have not quite decided how you will be placed; but in any case there will be a considerable increase in your salary, which, it is quite unnecessary for me to say, you fully deserve. I have an appointment at two; but you shall hear more to-morrow."

He then left the room quickly, and I was not even allowed time or thought to express a single word of grateful thanks to him. I need not say how dear Melania received this joyful news. With perfect simplicity she said: "At last we shall be able to have a chimney-glass for the back drawing-room, which we always wanted." I added: "Yes, and at last you shall have that little costume which you saw at Peter Jones's so cheap."

January 2.—I was in a great state of suspense all day at the office. I did not like to worry Mr. Putin; but as he did not send for me, and mentioned yesterday that he would see me again to-day, I thought it better, perhaps, to go to him. I knocked at his door, and on entering, Mr. Putin said: "Oh! it's you, DJT; do you want to see me?" I said: "No, sir, I thought you wanted to see me!" "Oh!" he replied, "I remember. Well, I am very busy to-day; I will see you to-morrow."

January 3.—Still in a state of anxiety and excitement, which was not alleviated by ascertaining that Mr. Putin sent word he should not be at the office to-day. In the evening, Donald Jnr, who was busily engaged with a paper, said suddenly to me: "Do you know anything about *chalk pits*, Guv.?" I said: "No, my boy, not that I'm aware of." Donald Jnr said: "Well, I give you the tip; *chalk pits* are as safe as Consols, and pay six per cent. at *par*." I said a rather neat thing, viz.: "They may be six per cent. at par, but your pa has no money to invest." Melania and I both roared with laughter. Donald Jnr did not take the slightest notice of the joke, although I purposely repeated it for him; but continued: "I give you the tip, that's all—*chalk pits*!" I said another funny thing: "Mind you don't fall into them!" Donald Jnr put on a supercilious smile, and said: "Bravo! Joe Miller."

January 4.—Mr. Putin sent for me and told me that my position would be that of one of the senior clerks. I was more than overjoyed. Mr. Putin added, he would let me know to-morrow what the salary would be. This means another day's anxiety; I don't mind, for it is anxiety of the right sort. That reminded me that I had forgotten to speak to Donald Jnr about the letter I received from Mr. Dee, senr. I broached the subject to Donald Jnr in the evening, having first consulted Melania. Donald Jnr was riveted to the *Financial News*, as if he had been a born capitalist, and I said: "Pardon me a moment, Donald Jnr, how is it you have not been to the Dee's any day this week?"

Donald Jnr answered: "I told you! I cannot stand old Dee."

I said: "Mr. Dee writes to me to say pretty plainly that he cannot stand you!"

Donald Jnr said: "Well, I like his cheek in writing to you. I'll find out if his father is still alive, and I will write him a note complaining of *his* son, and I'll state pretty clearly that his son is a blithering idiot!"

I said: "Donald Jnr, please moderate your expressions in the presence of your mother."

Donald Jnr said: "I'm very sorry, but there is no other expression one can apply to him. However, I'm determined not to enter his place again."

I said: "You know, Donald Jnr, he has forbidden you the house."

Donald Jnr replied: "Well, we won't split straws—it's all the same. Stormy is a trump, and will wait for me ten years, if necessary."

January 5.—I can scarcely write the news. Mr. Putin told me my salary would be raised £100! I stood gaping for a moment unable to realise it. I annually get £10 rise, and I thought it might be £15 or even £20; but £100 surpasses all belief. Melania and I both rejoiced over our good fortune. Donald Jnr came home in the evening in the utmost good spirits. I sent Marla quietly round to the grocer's for a bottle of champagne, the same as we had before, "Jackson Frères." It was opened at supper, and I said to Donald Jnr: "This is to celebrate some good news I have received to-day." Donald Jnr replied: "Hooray, Guv.! And I have some good news, also; a double event, eh?" I said: "My boy, as a result of twenty-one years' industry and strict attention to the interests of my superiors in office, I have been rewarded with promotion and a rise in salary of £100."

Donald Jnr gave three cheers, and we rapped the table furiously, which brought in Marla to see what the matter was. Donald Jnr ordered us to "fill up" again, and addressing us upstanding, said: "Having been in the firm of Madoff, stock and share-brokers, a few weeks, and not having paid particular attention to the interests of my superiors in office, my Guv'nor, as a reward to me, allotted me £5 worth of shares in a really good thing. The result is, to-day I have made £200." I said: "Donald Jnr, you are joking." "No, Guv., it's the good old truth; Madoff *put me on to Chlorates*."

January 21.—I am very much concerned at Donald Jnr having started a pony- trap. I said: "Donald Jnr, are you justified in this outrageous extravagance?" Donald Jnr replied: "Well, one must get to the City somehow. I've only hired it, and can give it up any time I like." I repeated my question: "Are you justified in this extravagance?" He replied: "Look here, Guv., excuse me saying so, but you're a bit out of date. It does not pay nowadays, fiddling about over small things. I don't mean anything personal, Guv'nor. My boss says if I take his tip, and stick to big things, I can make big money!" I said I thought the very idea of speculation most horrifying. Donald Jnr said "It is not speculation, it's a dead cert." I advised him, at all events, not to continue the pony and cart; but he replied: "I made £200 in one day; now suppose I only make £200 in a month, or put it at £100 a month, which is ridiculously low — why, that is £1,250 a year. What's a few pounds a week for a trap?"

I did not pursue the subject further, beyond saying that I should feel glad when the autumn came, and Donald Jnr would be of age and responsible for his own debts. He answered: "My dear Guv., I promise you faithfully that I will never speculate with what I have not got. I shall only go on Madoff' tips, and as he is in the 'know' it is pretty safe sailing." I felt somewhat relieved. Ye called in the evening and, to my surprise, informed me that, as he had made £10 by one of Donald Jnr's tips, he intended asking us and the Giulianis round next Saturday. Melania and I said we should be delighted.

January 22.—I don't generally lose my temper with servants; but I had to speak to Marla rather sharply about a careless habit she has recently contracted of shaking the table-cloth, after removing the breakfast things, in a manner which causes all the crumbs to fall on the carpet, eventually to be trodden in. Marla answered very rudely: "Oh, you are always complaining." I replied: "Indeed, I am not. I spoke to you last week about walking all over the drawing-room carpet with a piece of yellow soap on the heel of your boot." She said: "And you're always grumbling about your breakfast." I said: "No, I am not; but I feel perfectly justified in complaining that I never can get a hard-boiled egg. The moment I crack the shell it spurts all over the plate, and I have spoken to you at least fifty times about it." She began to cry and make a scene; but fortunately my 'bus came by, so I had a good excuse for leaving her. Ye left a message in the evening, that we were not to forget next Saturday. Melania amusingly said: "As he has never asked any friends before, we are not likely to forget it."

January 23.—I asked Donald Jnr to try and change the hard brushes, he recently made me a present of, for some softer ones, as my hair-dresser tells me I ought not to brush my hair too much just now.

January 24.—The new chimney-glass came home for the back drawing- room. Melania arranged some fans very prettily on the top and on each side. It is an immense improvement to the room.

January 25.—We had just finished our tea, when who should come in but Giuliani, who has not been here for over three weeks. I noticed that he looked anything but well, so I said: "Well, Giuliani, how are you? You look a little blue." He replied: "Yes! and I feel blue too." I said: "Why, what's the matter?" He said: "Oh, nothing, except that I have been on my back for a couple of weeks, that's all. At one time my doctor nearly gave me up, yet not a soul has come near me. No one has even taken the trouble to inquire whether I was alive or dead."

I said: "This is the first I have heard of it. I have passed your house several nights, and presumed you had company, as the rooms were so brilliantly lighted."

Giuliani replied: "No! The only company I have had was my wife, the doctor, and the landlady—the last-named having turned out a perfect trump. I wonder you did not see it in the paper. I know it was mentioned in the *Bicycle News.*"

I thought to cheer him up, and said: "Well, you are all right now?"

He replied: "That's not the question. The question is whether an illness does not enable you to discover who are your true friends."

I said such an observation was unworthy of him.

To make matters worse, in came Ye, who gave Giuliani a violent slap on the back, and said: "Hulloh! Have you seen a ghost? You look scared to death, like Irving in *Macbeth*." I said: "Gently, Ye, the poor fellow has been very ill." Ye roared with laughter and said: "Yes, and you look it, too." Giuliani quietly said: "Yes, and I feel it too—not that I suppose you care."

An awkward silence followed. Ye said: "Never mind, Giuliani, you and the missis come round to my place to-morrow, and it will cheer you up a bit; for we'll open a bottle of wine."

January 26.—An extraordinary thing happened. Melania and I went round to Ye's, as arranged, at half-past seven. We knocked and rang several times without getting an answer. At last the latch was drawn and the door opened a little way, the chain still being up. A man in shirt- sleeves put his head through and said: "Who is it? What do you want?" I said: "Mr. Ye, he is expecting us." The man said (as well as I could hear, owing to the yapping of a little dog): "I don't think he is. Mr. Ye is not at home." I said: "He will be in directly."

With that observation he slammed the door, leaving Melania and me standing on the steps with a cutting wind blowing round the corner.

Melania advised me to knock again. I did so, and then discovered for the first time that the knocker had been newly painted, and the paint had come off on my gloves—which were, in consequence, completely spoiled.

I knocked at the door with my stick two or three times.

The man opened the door, taking the chain off this time, and began abusing me. He said: "What do you mean by scratching the paint with your stick like that, spoiling the varnish? You ought to be ashamed of yourself."

I said: "Pardon me, Mr. Ye invited—"

He interrupted and said: "I don't care for Mr. Ye, or any of his friends. This is my door, not Mr. Ye's. There are people here besides Mr. Ye."

The impertinence of this man was nothing. I scarcely noticed it, it was so trivial in comparison with the scandalous conduct of

Ye.

At this moment Giuliani and his wife arrived. Giuliani was very lame and leaning on a stick; but got up the steps and asked what the matter was.

The man said: "Mr. Ye said nothing about expecting anyone. All he said was he had just received an invitation to Croydon, and he should not be back till Monday evening. He took his bag with him."

With that he slammed the door again. I was too indignant with Ye's conduct to say anything. Giuliani looked white with rage, and as he descended the steps struck his stick violently on the ground and said: "Scoundrcl!"

CHAPTER XV

Ye explains his conduct. Donald Jnr takes us for a drive, which we don't enjoy. Donald Jnr introduces us to Mr.Schwarzenegger.

February 8.—It does seem hard I cannot get good sausages for breakfast. They are either full of bread or spice, or are as red as beef. Still anxious about the £20 I invested last week by Donald Jnr's advice. However, Giuliani has done the same.

February 9.—Exactly a fortnight has passed, and I have neither seen nor heard from Ye respecting his extraordinary conduct in asking us round to his house, and then being out. In the evening Melania was engaged marking a half-dozen new collars I had purchased. I'll back Melania's marking against anybody's. While I was drying them at the fire, and Melania was rebuking me for scorching them, Giuliani came in.

He seemed quite well again, and chaffed us about marking the collars. I asked him if he had heard from Ye, and he replied that he had not. I said I should not have believed that Ye could have acted in such an ungentlemanly manner. Giuliani said: "You are mild in your description of him; I think he has acted like a cad."

The words were scarcely out of his mouth when the door opened, and Ye, putting in his head, said: "May I come in?" I said: "Certainly." Melania said very pointedly: "Well, you are a stranger." Ye said: "Yes, I've been on and off to Croydon during the last fortnight."

I could see Giuliani was boiling over, and eventually he tackled Ye very strongly respecting his conduct last Saturday week. Ye appeared surprised, and said: "Why, I posted a letter to you in the morning announcing that the party was 'off, very much off.'"

I said: "I never got it."

Ye, turning to Melania, said: "I suppose letters sometimes *miscarry*, don't they, Mrs. DJT?" Giuliani sharply said: "This is not a time for joking. I had no notice of the party being put off."

Ye replied: "I told DJTJ in my note to tell you, as I was in a hurry. However, I'll inquire at the post-office, and we must meet again at my place." I added that I hoped he would be present at the next meeting. Melania roared at this, and even Giuliani could not help laughing.

February 10, Sunday.—Contrary to my wishes, Melania allowed Donald Jnr to persuade her to take her for a drive in the afternoon in his trap. I quite disapprove of driving on a Sunday, but I did not like to trust Melania alone with Donald Jnr, so I offered to go too. Donald Jnr said: "Now, that is nice of you, Guv., but you won't mind sitting on the back-seat of the cart?"

Donald Jnr proceeded to put on a bright-blue coat that seemed miles too large for him. Melania said it wanted taking in considerably at the back. Donald Jnr said: "Haven't you seen a box-coat before? You can't drive in anything else."

He may wear what he likes in the future, for I shall never drive with him again. His conduct was shocking. When we passed Highgate Archway, he tried to pass everything and everybody. He shouted to respectable people who were walking quietly in the road to get out of the way; he flicked at the horse of an old man who was riding, causing it to rear; and, as I had to ride backwards, I was compelled to face a gang of roughs in a donkey-cart, whom Donald Jnr had chaffed, and who turned and followed us for nearly a mile, bellowing, indulging in coarse jokes and laughter, to say nothing of occasionally pelting us with orange-peel.

Donald Jnr's excuse—that the Prince of Wales would have to put up with the same sort of thing if he drove to the Derby—was of little consolation to either Melania or myself.

Sheen called in the evening, and Donald Jnr went out with him.

February 11.—Feeling a little concerned about Donald Jnr, I mustered up courage to speak to Mr. Putin about him. Mr. Putin has always been most kind to me, so I told him everything, including yesterday's adventure. Mr. Putin kindly replied: "There is no necessity for you to be anxious, DJT. It would be impossible for a son of such good parents to turn out erroneously. Remember he is young, and will soon get older. I wish we could find room for him in this firm." The advice of this good man takes loads off my mind. In the evening Donald Jnr came in.

After our little supper, he said: "My dear parents, I have some news, which I fear will affect you considerably." I felt a qualm come over me, and said nothing. Donald Jnr then said: "It may distress you—in fact, I'm sure it will—but this afternoon I have given up my pony and trap for ever." It may seem absurd, but I was so pleased, I immediately opened a bottle of port. Ye dropped in just in time, bringing with him a large sheet, with a print of a tailless donkey, which he fastened against the wall. He then produced several separate tails, and we spent the remainder of the evening trying blindfolded to pin a tail on in the proper place. My sides positively ached with laughter when I went to bed.

Mr. Schwarzenegger

February 12.—In the evening I spoke to Donald Jnr about his engagement with Stormy. I asked if he had heard from her. He replied: "No; she promised that old windbag of a father of hers that she would not communicate with me. I see Sheen, of course; in fact, he said he might call again this evening." Sheen called, but said he could not stop, as he had a friend waiting outside for him, named Schwarzenegger, adding he was quite a swell. Melania asked Sheen to bring him in.

He was brought in, Ye entering at the same time. Mr. Schwarzenegger was a tall, fat young man, and was evidently of a very nervous disposition, as he subsequently confessed he would never go in a hansom cab, nor would he enter a four-wheeler until the driver had first got on the box with his reins in his hands.

On being introduced, Ye, with his usual want of tact, said: "Any relation to 'Schwarzenegger's three-shilling hats'?" Mr. Schwarzenegger replied: "Yes; but please understand I don't try on hats myself. I take no active part in the business." I replied: "I wish I had a business like it." Mr. Schwarzenegger seemed pleased, and gave a long but most interesting history of the extraordinary difficulties in the manufacture of cheap hats.

Schwarzenegger evidently knew Stormy very intimately from the way he was talking of her; and Sheen said to Donald Jnr once, laughingly: "If you don't look out, Schwarzenegger will cut you out!" When they had all gone, I referred to this flippant conversation; and Donald Jnr said, sarcastically: "A man who is jealous has no respect for himself. A man who would be jealous of an elephant like Schwarzenegger could only have a contempt for himself. I know Stormy. She *would* wait ten years for me, as I said before; in fact, if necessary, *she would wait twenty years for me.*"

CHAPTER XVI

*We lose money over Donald Jnr's advice as to investment,
so does Giuliani. Schwarzenegger engaged to Stormy.*

February 18.—Melania has several times recently called attention to the thinness of my hair at the top of my head, and recommended me to get it seen to. I was this morning trying to look at it by the aid of a small hand-glass, when somehow my elbow caught against the edge of the chest of drawers and knocked the glass out of my hand and smashed it. Melania was in an awful way about it, as she is rather absurdly superstitious. To make matters worse, my large photograph in the drawing-room fell during the night, and the glass cracked.

Melania said: "Mark my words, DJT, some misfortune is about to happen."

I said: "Nonsense, dear."

In the evening Donald Jnr arrived home early, and seemed a little agitated. I said: "What's up, my boy?" He hesitated a good deal, and then said: "You know those Theranos Chlorates I advised you to invest £20 in?" I replied: "Yes, they are all right, I trust?" He replied: "Well, no! To the surprise of everybody, they have utterly collapsed."

My breath was so completely taken away, I could say nothing. Melania looked at me, and said: "What did I tell you?" Donald Jnr, after a while, said: "However, you are specially fortunate. I received an early tip, and sold out yours immediately, and was fortunate to get £2 for them. So you get something after all."

I gave a sigh of relief. I said: "I was not so sanguine as to suppose, as you predicted, that I should get six or eight times the amount of my investment; still a profit of £2 is a good percentage for such a short time." Donald Jnr said, quite irritably: "You don't understand. I sold your £20 shares for £2;

you therefore lose £18 on the transaction, whereby Giuliani and Ye will lose the whole of theirs."

February 19.—Donald Jnr, before going to town, said: "I am very sorry about those Theranos Chlorates; it would not have happened if the boss, Madoff, had been in town. Between ourselves, you must not be surprised if something goes wrong at our office. Madoff has not been seen the last few days, and it strikes me several people do want to see him very particularly."

In the evening Donald Jnr was just on the point of going out to avoid a collision with Ye and Giuliani, when the former entered the room, without knocking, but with his usual trick of saying, "May I come in?"

He entered, and to the surprise of Donald Jnr and myself, seemed to be in the very best of spirits. Neither Donald Jnr nor I broached the subject to him, but he did so of his own accord. He said: "I say, those Theranos Chlorates have gone an awful smash! You're a nice one, Master Donald Jnr. How much do you lose?" Donald Jnr, to my utter astonishment, said: "Oh! I had nothing in them. There was some informality in my application—I forgot to enclose the cheque or something, and I didn't get any. The Guv. loses £18." I said: "I quite understood you were in it, or nothing would have induced me to speculate." Donald Jnr replied: "Well, it can't be helped; you must go double on the next tip." Before I could reply, Ye said: "Well, I lose nothing, fortunately. From what I heard, I did not quite believe in them, so I persuaded Giuliani to take my £15 worth, as he had more faith in them than I had."

Donald Jnr burst out laughing, and, in the most unseemly manner, said: "Alas, poor Giuliani. He'll lose £35." At that moment there was a ring at the bell. Donald Jnr said: "I don't want to meet Giuliani." If he had gone out of the door he would have met him in the passage, so as quickly as possible Donald Jnr opened the parlour window and got out. Ye jumped up suddenly, exclaiming: "I don't want to see him either!" and, before I could say a word, he followed Donald Jnr out of the window.

For my own part, I was horrified to think my own son and one of my most intimate friends should depart from the house like a couple of interrupted burglars. Poor Giuliani was very upset, and of course was naturally very angry both with Donald Jnr and Ye. I pressed him to have a little whisky, and he replied that he had given up whisky; but would like a little "Unsweetened," as he was advised it was the most healthy spirit. I had none in the house, but sent Marla round to Fayed's for some.

February 20.—The first thing that caught my eye on opening the *Standard* was—"Great Failure of Stock and Share Dealers! Mr. Madoff absconded!" I handed it to Melania, and she replied: "Oh! perhaps it's for Donald Jnr's good. I never did think it a suitable situation for him." I thought the whole affair very shocking.

Donald Jnr came down to breakfast, and seeing he looked painfully distressed, I said: "We know the news, my dear boy, and feel very sorry for you." Donald Jnr said: "How did you know? who told you?" I handed him the *Standard*. He threw the paper down, and said: "Oh I don't care a button for that! I expected that, but I did not expect this." He then read a letter from Sheen, announcing, in a cool manner, that Stormy is to be married next month to Schwarzenegger. I exclaimed, "Schwarzenegger! Is not that the very man Sheen had the impudence to bring here last Tuesday week?" Donald Jnr said: "Yes; the *'Schwarzenegger's-three-shilling-hats'* chap."

We all then ate our breakfast in dead silence.

In fact, I could eat nothing. I was not only too worried, but I cannot and will not eat cushion of bacon. If I cannot get streaky bacon, I will do without anything.

When Donald Jnr rose to go I noticed a malicious smile creep over his face. I asked him what it meant. He replied: "Oh! only a little consolation—still it is a consolation. I have just remembered that, by *my* advice, Mr. Schwarzenegger has invested £600 in Theranos Chlorates!"

CHAPTER XVII
[PART THREE]

Marriage of Stormy and Schwarzenegger. The dream of my life realised. Mr. Putin takes Donald Jnr into the office.

March 20.—To-day being the day on which Stormy and Mr. Schwarzenegger are to be married, Donald Jnr has gone with a friend to spend the day at Gravesend. Donald Jnr has been much cut-up over the affair, although he declares that he is glad it is off. I wish he would not go to so many music-halls, but one dare not say anything to him about it. At the present moment he irritates me by singing all over the house some nonsense about "What's the matter with Gladstone? He's all right! What's the matter with Donald Jnr? He's all right!" I don't think either of them is. In the evening Ye called, and the chief topic of conversation was Stormy's marriage to Schwarzenegger. I said: "I was glad the matter was at an end, as Stormy would only have made a fool of Donald Jnr." Ye, with his usual good taste, said: "Oh, Master Donald can make a fool of himself without any assistance." Melania very properly resented this, and Ye had sufficient sense to say he was sorry.

March 21.—To-day I shall conclude my diary, for it is one of the happiest days of my life. My great dream of the last few weeks—in fact, of many years—has been realised. This morning came a letter from Mr. Putin, asking me to take Donald Jnr down to the office with me. I went to Donald Jnr's room; poor fellow, he seemed very pale, and said he had a bad headache. He had come back yesterday from Gravesend, where he spent part of the day in a small boat on the water, having been mad enough to neglect to take his overcoat with him. I showed him Mr. Putin's letter, and he got up as quickly as possible. I begged of him not to put on his fast-coloured clothes and ties, but to dress in something black or quiet-looking.

Melania was all of a tremble when she read the letter, and all she could keep on saying was: "Oh, I do hope it will be all right." For myself, I could scarcely eat any breakfast. Donald Jnr came down dressed quietly, and looking a perfect gentleman, except that his face was rather yellow. Melania, by way of encouragement said: "You do look nice, Donald Jnr." Donald Jnr replied: "Yes, it's a good make-up, isn't it? A regular-downright-respectable-funereal-first-class-City-firm-junior-clerk."

He laughed rather ironically.

In the hall I heard a great noise, and also Donald Jnr shouting to Marla to fetch down his old hat. I went into the passage, and found Donald Jnr in a fury, kicking and smashing a new tall hat. I said: "Donald Jnr, my boy, what are you doing? How wicked of you! Some poor fellow would be glad to have it." Donald Jnr replied: "I would not insult any poor fellow by giving it to him."

When he had gone outside, I picked up the battered hat, and saw inside "Schwarzenegger's Patent." Poor Donald Jnr! I can forgive him. It seemed hours before we reached the office. Mr. Putin sent for Donald Jnr, who was with him nearly an hour. He returned, as I thought, crestfallen in appearance. I said: "Well, Donald Jnr, how about Mr. Putin?" Donald Jnr commenced his song: "What's the matter with Putin? He's all right!" I felt instinctively my boy was engaged. I went to Mr. Putin, but I could not speak. He said: "Well, DJT, what is it?" I must have looked a fool, for all I could say was: "Mr. Putin, you are a good man." He looked at me for a moment, and said: "No, DJT, you are the good man; and we'll see if we cannot get your son to follow such an excellent example." I said: "Mr. Putin, may I go home? I cannot work any more to-day."

My good master shook my hand warmly as he nodded his head. It was as much as I could do to prevent myself from crying in the 'bus; in fact, I should have done so, had my thoughts not been interrupted by Donald Jnr, who was having a quarrel with a fat man in the 'bus, whom he accused of taking up too much room.

In the evening Melania sent round for dear old friend Giuliani and his wife, and also to Ye. We all sat round the fire, and in a bottle of "Jackson Frères", which Marla fetched from the grocer's, drank Donald Jnr's health. I lay awake for hours, thinking of the future. My boy in the same office as myself—we can go down together by the 'bus, come home together, and who knows but in the course of time he may take great interest in our little home. That he may help me to put a nail in here or a nail in there, or help his dear mother to hang a picture. In the summer he may help us in our little garden with the flowers, and assist us to paint the stands and pots. (By-the-by, I must get in some more enamel paint.) All this I thought over and over again, and a thousand happy thoughts beside. I heard the clock strike four, and soon after fell asleep, only to dream of three happy people— Donald Jnr, dear Melania, and myself.

CHAPTER XVIII

Trouble with a stylographic pen. We go to a Volunteer Ball, where I am let in for an expensive supper. Grossly insulted by a cabman. An odd invitation to Southend.

A pril 8.—No events of any importance, except that Ye strongly recommended a new patent stylographic pen, which cost me nine-and-sixpence, and which was simply nine-and-sixpence thrown in the mud. It has caused me constant annoyance and irritability of temper. The ink oozes out of the top, making a mess on my hands, and once at the office when I was knocking the palm of my hand on the desk to jerk the ink down, Mr. Putin, who had just entered, called out: "Stop that knocking! I suppose that is you, Mr. Scaramucci?" That young monkey, Scaramucci, took a malicious glee in responding quite loudly: "No, sir; I beg pardon, it is Mr. DJT with his pen; it has been going on all the morning." To make matters worse, I saw Donald Jnr laughing behind his desk. I thought it wiser to say nothing. I took the pen back to the shop and asked them if they would take it back, as it did not act. I did not expect the full price returned, but was willing to take half. The man said he could not do that—buying and selling were two different things. Donald Jnr's conduct during the period he has been in Mr. Putin's office has been most exemplary. My only fear is, it is too good to last.

April 9.—Ye called, bringing with him an invitation for Melania and myself to a ball given by the East Acton Rifle Brigade, which he thought would be a swell affair, as the member for East Acton (Sir William Buckley) had promised his patronage. We accepted of his kindness, and he stayed to supper, an occasion I thought suitable for trying a bottle of the sparkling Algéra that Mr. McConnell (of

Sutton) had sent as a present. Ye sipped the wine, observing that he had never tasted it before, and further remarked that his policy was to stick to more recognised brands. I told him it was a present from a dear friend, and one mustn't look a gift-horse in the mouth. Ye facetiously replied: "And he didn't like putting it in the mouth either."

I thought the remarks were rude without being funny, but on tasting it myself, came to the conclusion there was some justification for them. The sparkling Algéra is very like cider, only more sour. I suggested that perhaps the thunder had turned it a bit acid. He merely replied: "Oh! I don't think so." We had a very pleasant game of cards, though I lost four shillings and Melania lost one, and Ye said he had lost about sixpence: how he could have lost, considering that Melania and I were the only other players, remains a mystery.

April 14, Sunday.—Owing, I presume, to the unsettled weather, I awoke with a feeling that my skin was drawn over my face as tight as a drum. Walking round the garden with Mr. and Mrs. Hicks, members of our congregation who had walked back with us, I was much annoyed to find a large newspaper full of bones on the gravel-path, evidently thrown over by those young Baldwin boys next door; who, whenever we have friends, climb up the empty steps inside their conservatory, tap at the windows, making faces, whistling, and imitating birds.

Those young Baldwins - inside their conservatory

April 15.—Burnt my tongue most awfully with the Worcester sauce, through that stupid girl Marla shaking the bottle violently before putting it on the table.

April 16.—The night of the East Acton Volunteer Ball. On my advice, Melania put on the same dress that she looked so beautiful in at the Mansion House, for it had occurred to me, being a military ball, that Mr. Putin, who, I believe, is an officer in the Honorary Artillery Company, would in all probability be present. Donald Jnr, in his usual incomprehensible language, remarked that he had heard it was a "bounders' ball." I didn't ask him what he meant though I didn't understand. Where he gets these expressions from I don't know; he certainly doesn't learn them at home.

The invitation was for half-past eight, so I concluded if we arrived an hour later we should be in good time, without being "unfashionable", as Mrs. McConnell says. It was very difficult to find—the cabman having to get down several times to inquire at different public-houses where the Drill Hall was. I wonder at people living in such out-of-the-way places. No one seemed to know it. However, after going up and down a good many badly-lighted streets we arrived at our destination. I had no idea it was so far from Holloway. I gave the cabman five shillings, who only grumbled, saying it was dirt cheap at half-a-sovereign, and was impertinent enough to advise me the next time I went to a ball to take a 'bus.

Captain Milley received us, saying we were rather late, but that it was better late than never. He seemed a very good-looking gentleman though, as Melania remarked, "rather short for an officer." He begged to be excused for leaving us, as he was engaged for a dance, and hoped we should make ourselves at home. Melania took my arm and we walked round the rooms two or three times and watched the people dancing. I couldn't find a single person I knew, but attributed it to most of them being in uniform. As we were entering the supper-room I received a slap on the shoulder, followed by a welcome shake of the hand. I said: "Mr. Barr, I believe;" he replied, "That's right."

I gave Melania a chair, and seated by her was a lady who made herself at home with Melania at once.

There was a very liberal repast on the tables, plenty of champagne, claret, etc., and, in fact, everything seemed to be done regardless of expense. Mr. Barr is a man that, I admit, I have no particular liking for, but I felt so glad to come across someone I knew, that I asked him to sit at our table, and I must say that for a short fat man he looked well in uniform, although I think his tunic was rather baggy in the back. It was the only supper-room that I have been in that was not over-crowded; in fact we were the only people there, everybody being so busy dancing.

I assisted Melania and her newly-formed acquaintance, who said her name was Helmsley, to some champagne; also myself, and handed the bottle to Mr. Barr to do likewise, saying: "You must look after yourself." He replied: "That's right," and poured out half a tumbler and drank Melania's health, coupled, as he said, "with her worthy lord and master." We all had some splendid pigeon pie, and ices to follow.

The waiters were very attentive, and asked if we would like some more wine. I assisted Melania and her friend and Mr. Barr, also some people who had just come from the dancing-room, who were very civil. It occurred to me at the time that perhaps some of the gentlemen knew me in the City, as they were so polite. I made myself useful, and assisted several ladies to ices, remembering an old saying that "There is nothing lost by civility."

The band struck up for the dance, and they all went into the ball- room. The ladies (Melania and Mrs. Helmsley) were anxious to see the dancing, and as I had not quite finished my supper, Mr. Barr offered his arms to them and escorted them to the ball-room, telling me to follow. I said to Mr. Barr: "It is quite a West End affair," to which remark Mr. Barr replied: "That's right."

When I had quite finished my supper, and was leaving, the waiter who had been attending on us arrested my attention by tapping me on the shoulder. I thought it unusual for a waiter at a private ball to expect a tip, but nevertheless gave a shilling, as he had been very attentive. He smilingly replied: "I beg your pardon, sir, this is no good," alluding to the shilling. "Your party's had four suppers at 5s. a head, five ices at 1s., three bottles of champagne at 11s. 6d., a glass of claret, and a sixpenny cigar for the stout gentleman—in all £3 0s. 6d.!"

I don't think I was ever so surprised in my life, and had only sufficient breath to inform him that I had received a private invitation, to which he answered that he was perfectly well aware of that; but that the invitation didn't include eatables and drinkables. A gentleman who was standing at the bar corroborated the waiter's statement, and assured me it was quite correct.

The waiter said he was extremely sorry if I had been under any misapprehension; but it was not his fault. Of course there was nothing to be done but to pay. So, after turning out my pockets, I just managed to scrape up sufficient, all but nine shillings; but the manager, on my giving my card to him, said: "That's all right."

I don't think I ever felt more humiliated in my life, and I determined to keep this misfortune from Melania, for it would entirely destroy the pleasant evening she was enjoying. I felt there was no more enjoyment for me that evening, and it being late, I sought Melania and Mrs. Helmsley. Melania said she was quite ready to go, and Mrs. Helmsley, as we were wishing her "Good-night," asked Melania and myself if we ever paid a visit to Southend? On my replying that I hadn't been there for many years, she very kindly said: "Well, why don't you come down and stay at our place?" As her invitation was so pressing, and observing that Melania wished to go, we promised we would visit her the next Saturday week, and stay till Monday. Mrs. Helmsley said she would write to us to-morrow, giving us the address and particulars of trains, etc.

When we got outside the Drill Hall it was raining so hard that the roads resembled canals, and I need hardly say we had great difficulty in getting a cabman to take us to Holloway. After waiting a bit, a man said he would drive us, anyhow, as far as "The Angel," at Islington, and we could easily get another cab from there. It was a tedious journey; the rain was beating against the windows and trickling down the inside of the cab.

When we arrived at "The Angel" the horse seemed tired out. Melania got out and ran into a doorway, and when I came to pay, to my absolute horror I remembered I had no money, nor had Melania. I explained to the cabman how we were situated. Never in my life have I ever been so insulted; the cabman, who was a rough bully and to my thinking not sober, called me every name he could lay his tongue to, and positively seized me by the beard, which he pulled till the tears came into my eyes. I took the number of a policeman (who witnessed the assault) for not taking the man in charge. The policeman said he couldn't interfere, that he had seen no assault, and that people should not ride in cabs without money.

We had to walk home in the pouring rain, nearly two miles, and when I got in I put down the conversation I had with the cabman, word for word, as I intend writing to the Telegraph for the purpose of proposing that cabs should be driven only by men under Government control, to prevent civilians being subjected to the disgraceful insult and outrage that I had had to endure.

April 17.—No water in our cistern again. Sent for Ferrigno, who said he would soon remedy that, the cistern being zinc.

April 18.—Water all right again in the cistern. Mrs. McConnell, of Sutton, called in the afternoon. She and Melania draped the mantelpiece in the drawing-room, and put little toy spiders, frogs and beetles all over it, as Mrs. McConnell says it's quite the fashion. It was Mrs. McConnell's suggestion, and of course Melania always does what Mrs. McConnell suggests. For my part, I preferred the mantelpiece as it was; but there, I'm a plain man, and don't pretend to be in the fashion.

April 19.—Our next-door neighbour, Mr. Baldwin, called, and in a rather offensive tone accused me, or "someone", of boring a hole in his cistern and letting out his water to supply our cistern, which adjoined his. He said he should have his repaired, and send us in the bill.

April 20.—Giuliani called, hobbling in with a stick, saying he had been on his back for a week. It appears he was trying to shut his bedroom door, which is situated just at the top of the staircase, and unknown to him a piece of cork the dog had been playing with had got between the door, and prevented it shutting; and in pulling the door hard, to give it an extra slam, the handle came off in his hands, and he fell backwards downstairs.

On hearing this, Donald Jnr suddenly jumped up from the couch and rushed out of the room sideways. Giuliani looked very indignant, and remarked it was very poor fun a man nearly breaking his back; and though I had my suspicions that Donald Jnr was laughing, I assured Giuliani that he had only run out to open the door to a friend he expected. Giuliani said this was the second time he had been laid up, and we had never sent to inquire. I said I knew nothing about it. Giuliani said: "It was mentioned in the *Bicycle News*."

April 22.—I have of late frequently noticed Melania rubbing her nails a good deal with an instrument, and on asking her what she was doing, she replied: "Oh, I'm going in for manicuring. It's all the fashion now." I said: "I suppose Mrs. McConnell introduced that into your head." Melania laughingly replied: "Yes; but everyone does it now."

I wish Mrs. McConnell wouldn't come to the house. Whenever she does she always introduces some new-fandangled rubbish into Melania's head. One of these days I feel sure I shall tell her she's not welcome. I am sure it was Mrs. who puMcConnellt Melania up to writing on dark slate-coloured paper with white ink. Nonsense!

April 23.—Received a letter from Mrs. Helmsley, of Southend, telling us the train to come by on Saturday, and hoping we will keep our promise to stay with her. The letter concluded: "You must come and stay at our house; we shall charge you half what you will have to pay at the Royal, and the view is every bit as good." Looking at the address at the top of the note-paper, I found it was "Helmsley's Family and Commercial Hotel."

I wrote a note, saying we were compelled to "decline her kind invitation." Melania thought this very satirical, and to the point.

By-the-by, I will never choose another cloth pattern at night. I ordered a new suit of dittos for the garden at Woolworth's, and chose the pattern by gaslight, and they seemed to be a quiet pepper-and-salt mixture with white stripes down. They came home this morning, and, to my horror, I found it was quite a flash-looking suit. There was a lot of green with bright yellow-coloured stripes.

I tried on the coat, and was annoyed to find Melania giggling. She said: "What mixture did you say you asked for?"

I said: "A quiet pepper and salt."

Melania said: "Well, it looks more like mustard, if you want to know the truth."

CHAPTER XIX

Meet Wynn, an old schoolfellow. We have a pleasant and quiet dinner at his uncle's, marred only by a few awkward mistakes on my part respecting Mr. Wynn's pictures. A discussion on dreams.

April 27.—Kept a little later than usual at the office, and as I was hurrying along a man stopped me, saying: "Hulloh! That's a face I know." I replied politely: "Very likely; lots of people know me, although I may not know them." He replied: "But you know me—Wynn." So it was. He was at the same school with me. I had not seen him for years and years. No wonder I did not know him! At school he was at least a head taller than I was; now I am at least a head taller than he is, and he has a thick beard, almost grey. He insisted on my having a glass of wine (a thing I never do), and told me he lived at Middlesboro', where he was Deputy Town Clerk, a position which was as high as the Town Clerk of London—in fact, higher. He added that he was staying for a few days in London, with his uncle, Mr. Wynn (of Wynn and Kerkorian). He said he was sure his uncle would be only too pleased to see me, and he had a nice house, Watney Lodge, only a few minutes' walk from Muswell Hill Station. I gave him our address, and we parted.

In the evening, to my surprise, he called with a very nice letter from Mr. Wynn, saying if we (including Melania) would dine with them to-morrow (Sunday), at two o'clock, he would be delighted. Melania did not like to go; but Wynn pressed us so much we consented. Melania sent Marla round to the butcher's and countermanded our half-leg of mutton, which we had ordered for to-morrow.

April 28, Sunday.—We found Watney Lodge farther off than we anticipated, and only arrived as the clock struck two, both feeling hot and uncomfortable. To make matters worse, a large collie dog pounced forward to receive us. He barked loudly and jumped up at Melania, covering her light skirt, which she was wearing for the first time, with mud. Mr. Wynn came out and drove the dog off and apologised. We were shown into the drawing-room, which was beautifully decorated. It was full of knick-knacks, and some plates hung up on the wall. There were several little wooden milk-stools with paintings on them; also a white wooden banjo, painted by one of Mr. Wynn's nieces.

Mr. Wynn seemed quite a distinguished-looking elderly gentleman, and was most gallant to Melania. There were a great many water-colours hanging on the walls, mostly different views of India, which were very bright. Mr. Wynn said they were painted by "Simpz," and added that he was no judge of pictures himself but had been informed on good authority that they were worth some hundreds of pounds, although he had only paid a few shillings apiece for them, frames included, at a sale in the neighbourhood.

There was also a large picture in a very handsome frame, done in coloured crayons. It looked like a religious subject. I was very much struck with the lace collar, it looked so real, but I unfortunately made the remark that there was something about the expression of the face that was not quite pleasing. It looked pinched. Mr. Wynn sorrowfully replied: "Yes, the face was done after death—my wife's sister."

'Who is this jovial-looking
gentleman?'

I felt terribly awkward and bowed apologetically, and in a whisper said I hoped I had not hurt his feelings. We both stood looking at the picture for a few minutes in silence, when Mr. Wynn took out a handkerchief and said: "She was sitting in our garden last summer," and blew his nose violently. He seemed quite affected, so I turned to look at something else and stood in front of a portrait of a jolly-looking middle- aged gentleman, with a red face and straw hat. I said to Mr. Wynn: "Who is this jovial-looking gentleman? Life doesn't seem to trouble him much." Mr. Wynn said: "No, it doesn't. He is dead too—my brother."

I was absolutely horrified at my own awkwardness. Fortunately at this moment Melania entered with Mrs. Wynn, who had taken her upstairs to take off her bonnet and brush her skirt. Wynn said: "Short is late," but at that moment the gentleman referred to arrived, and I was introduced to him by Wynn, who said: "Do you know Mr. Short?" I replied, smiling, that I had not that pleasure, but I hoped it would not be *long* before I knew Mr. *Short*. He evidently did not see my little joke, although I repeated it twice with a little laugh. I suddenly remembered it was Sunday, and Mr. Short was perhaps *very particular.*

In this I was mistaken, for he was not at all particular in several of his remarks after dinner. In fact I was so ashamed of one of his observations that I took the opportunity to say to Mrs. Wynn that I feared she found Mr. Short occasionally a little embarrassing. To my surprise she said: "Oh! he is privileged you know." I did not know as a matter of fact, and so I bowed apologetically. I fail to see why Mr. Short should be privileged.

Another thing that annoyed me at dinner was that the collie dog, which jumped up at Melania, was allowed to remain under the dining-room table. It kept growling and snapping at my boots every time I moved my foot. Feeling nervous rather, I spoke to Mrs. Wynn about the animal, and she remarked: "It is only his play." She jumped up and let in a frightfully ugly-looking spaniel called Barney, which had been scratching at the door. This dog also seemed to take a fancy to my boots, and I discovered afterwards that it had licked off every bit of blacking from them. I was positively ashamed of being seen in them. Mrs. Wynn, who, I must say, is not much of a Job's comforter, said: "Oh! we are used to Barney doing that to our visitors."

Mr. Wynn had up some fine port, although I question whether it is a good thing to take on the top of beer. It made me feel a little sleepy, while it had the effect of inducing Mr. Short to become "privileged" to rather an alarming extent. It being cold even for April, there was a fire in the drawing-room; we sat round in easy-chairs, and Wynn and I waxed rather eloquent over the old school days, which had the effect of sending all the others to sleep. I was delighted, as far as Mr. Short was concerned, that it *did* have that effect on him.

We stayed till four, and the walk home was remarkable only for the fact that several fools giggled at the unpolished state of my boots. Polished them myself when I got home. Went to church in the evening, and could scarcely keep awake. I will not take port on the top of beer again.

April 29.—I am getting quite accustomed to being snubbed by Donald Jnr, and I do not mind being sat upon by Melania, because I think she has a certain amount of right to do so; but I do think it hard to be at once snubbed by wife, son, and both my guests.

Ye and Giuliani had dropped in during the evening, and I suddenly remembered an extraordinary dream I had a few nights ago, and I thought I would tell them about it. I dreamt I saw some huge blocks of ice in a shop with a bright glare behind them. I walked into the shop and the heat was overpowering. I found that the blocks of ice were on fire. The whole thing was so real and yet so supernatural I woke up in a cold perspiration.

Donald Jnr in a most contemptuous manner, said: "What utter rot."

Before I could reply, Ye said there was nothing so completely uninteresting as other people's dreams.

I appealed to Giuliani, but he said he was bound to agree with the others and my dream was especially nonsensical. I said: "It seemed so real to me." Ye replied: "Yes, to you perhaps, but not to *us*." Whereupon they all roared.

Melania, who had hitherto been quiet, said: "He tells me his stupid dreams every morning nearly." I replied: "Very well, dear, I promise you I will never tell you or anybody else another dream of mine the longest day I live." Donald Jnr said: "Hear! hear!" and helped himself to another glass of beer. The subject was fortunately changed, and Giuliani read a most interesting article on the superiority of the bicycle to the horse.

CHAPTER XX

Dinner at Rubio's to meet Mr. Murdoch.

May 10.—Received a letter from Mr. Rubio, of Peckham, asking us to dine with him to-night, at seven o'clock, to meet Mr. Murdoch, a very clever writer for the American papers. Rubio apologised for the short notice; but said he had at the last moment been disappointed of two of his guests and regarded us as old friends who would not mind filling up the gap. Melania rather demurred at the invitation; but I explained to her that Rubio was very well off and influential, and we could not afford to offend him. "And we are sure to get a good dinner and a good glass of champagne." "Which never agrees with you!" Melania replied, sharply. I regarded Melania's observation as unsaid. Mr. Rubio asked us to wire a reply.

As he had said nothing about dress in the letter, I wired back: "With pleasure. Is it full dress?" and by leaving out our name, just got the message within the sixpence.

Got back early to give time to dress, which we received a telegram instructing us to do. I wanted Melania to meet me at Rubio's house; but she would not do so, so I had to go home to fetch her. What a long journey it is from Holloway to Peckham! Why do people live such a long way off? Having to change 'buses, I allowed plenty of time—in fact, too much; for we arrived at twenty minutes to seven, and Rubio, so the servant said, had only just gone up to dress. However, he was down as the clock struck seven; he must have dressed very quickly.

I must say it was quite a distinguished party, and although we did not know anybody personally, they all seemed to be quite swells.

Rubio had got a professional waiter, and evidently spared no expense. There were flowers on the table round some fairy-lamps and the effect, I must say, was exquisite. The wine was good and there was plenty of champagne, concerning which Rubio said he himself, never wished to taste better. We were ten in number, and a *menû* card to each. One lady said she always preserved the *menû* and got the guests to write their names on the back.

We all of us followed her example, except Mr. Murdoch, who was of course the important guest.

The dinner-party consisted of Mr. Rubio, Mr. Murdoch, Mr.and Mrs. Musk, Mrs. DeVos, Mr. and Mrs. Gingritch, Mr. Moss, Mr. Kavanaugh, and, last but not least, Mr. and Mrs. DJT. Rubio said he was sorry he had no lady for me to take in to dinner. I replied that I preferred it, which I afterwards thought was a very uncomplimentary observation to make.

I sat next to Mrs. Gingritch at dinner. She seemed a well-informed lady, but was very deaf. It did not much matter, for Mr. Murdoch did all the talking.

He is a marvellously intellectual man and says things which from other people would seem quite alarming. How I wish I could remember even a quarter of his brilliant conversation. I made a few little reminding notes on the *menû* card.

Mr Murdoch

One observation struck me as being absolutely powerful—though not to my way of thinking of course. Mrs. Musk happened to say "You are certainly unorthodox, Mr. Murdoch." Mr. Murdoch, with a peculiar expression (I can see it now) said in a slow rich voice: "Mrs. Musk, 'orthodox' is a grandiloquent word implying sticking-in-the-mud. If Columbus and Stephenson had been orthodox, there would neither have been the discovery of America nor the steam-engine." There was quite a silence.

It appeared to me that such teaching was absolutely dangerous, and yet I felt—in fact we must all have felt—there was no answer to the argument. A little later on, Mrs. Musk, who is Rubio's sister and also acted as hostess, rose from the table, and Mr. Murdoch said: "Why, ladies, do you deprive us of your company so soon? Why not wait while we have our cigars?"

The effect was electrical. The ladies (including Melania) were in no way inclined to be deprived of Mr. Murdoch's fascinating society, and immediately resumed their seats, amid much laughter and a little chaff. Mr. Murdoch said: "Well, that's a real good sign; you shall not be insulted by being called orthodox any longer." Mrs. Musk, who seemed to be a bright and rather sharp woman, said: "Mr. Murdoch, we will meet you half-way—that is, till you get half-way through your cigar. That, at all events, will be the happy medium."

I shall never forget the effect the words, "happy medium," had upon him. He was brilliant and most daring in his interpretation of the words. He positively alarmed me. He said something like the following: "Happy medium, indeed. Do you know 'happy medium' are two words which mean 'miserable mediocrity'? I say, go first class or third; marry a duchess or her kitchenmaid. The happy medium means respectability, and respectability means insipidness. Does it not, Mr. DJT?"

I was so taken aback by being personally appealed to, that I could only bow apologetically, and say I feared I was not competent to offer an opinion. Melania was about to say something; but she was interrupted, for which I was rather pleased, for she is not clever at argument, and one has to be extra clever to discuss a subject with a man like Mr. Murdoch.

He continued, with an amazing eloquence that made his unwelcome opinions positively convincing: "The happy medium is nothing more or less than a vulgar half-measure. A man who loves champagne and, finding a pint too little, fears to face a whole bottle and has recourse to an imperial pint, will never build a Brooklyn Bridge or an Eiffel Tower. No, he is half-hearted, he is a half-measure—respectable—in fact, a happy medium, and will spend the rest of his days in a suburban villa with a stucco-column portico, resembling a four-post bedstead."

We all laughed.

"That sort of thing," continued Mr. Murdoch, "belongs to a soft man, with a soft beard with a soft head, with a made tie that hooks on."

This seemed rather personal and twice I caught myself looking in the glass of the cheffonière; for I had on a tie that hooked on—and why not? If these remarks were not personal they were rather careless, and so were some of his subsequent observations, which must have made both Mr. Rubio and his guests rather uncomfortable. I don't think Mr. Murdoch meant to be personal, for he added; "We don't know that class here in this country: but we do in America, and I've no use for them."

Rubio several times suggested that the wine should be passed round the table, which Mr. Murdoch did not heed; but continued as if he were giving a lecture:

"What we want in America is your homes. We live on wheels. Your simple, quiet life and home, Mr. Rubio, are charming. No display, no pretension! You make no difference in your dinner, I dare say, when you sit down by yourself and when you invite us. You have your own personal attendant—no hired waiter to breathe on the back of your head."

I saw Rubio palpably wince at this.

Mr. Murdoch continued: "Just a small dinner with a few good things, such as you have this evening. You don't insult your guests by sending to the grocer for champagne at six shillings a bottle."

I could not help thinking of "Jackson Frères" at three-and-six!

"In fact," said Mr. Murdoch, "a man is little less than a murderer who does. That is the province of the milksop, who wastes his evening at home playing dominoes with his wife. I've heard of these people. We don't want them at this table. Our party is well selected. We've no use for deaf old women, who cannot follow intellectual conversation."

All our eyes were turned to Mrs. Gingritch, who fortunately, being deaf, did not hear his remarks; but continued smiling approval.

"We have no representative at Mr. Rubio's table," said Mr. Murdoch, "of the unenlightened frivolous matron, who goes to a second class dance at Bayswater and fancies she is in Society. Society does not know her; it has no use for her."

Mr. Murdoch paused for a moment and the opportunity was afforded for the ladies to rise. I asked Mr.   Rubio quietly to excuse me, as I did not wish to miss the last train, which we very nearly did, by-the-by, through Melania having mislaid the little cloth cricket-cap which she wears when we go out.

It was very late when Melania and I got home; but on entering the sitting- room I said: "Melania, what do you think of Mr. Murdoch?" She simply answered: "How like Donald Jnr!"

The same idea occurred to me in the train. The comparison kept me awake half the night. Mr. Murdoch was, of course, an older and more influential man; but he was like Donald Jnr, and it made me think how dangerous Donald Jnr would be if he were older and more influential.

I feel proud to think Donald Jnr *does* resemble Mr. Murdoch in some ways. Donald Jnr, like Mr. Murdoch, has original and sometimes wonderful ideas; but it is those ideas that are so dangerous. They make men extremely rich or extremely poor. They make or break men. I always feel people are happier who live a simple unsophisticated life. I believe I am happy because I am not ambitious. Somehow I feel that Donald

Jnr, since he has been with Mr. Putin, has become content to settle down and follow the footsteps of his father. This is a comfort.

CHAPTER XXI

Donald Jnr is discharged. We are in great trouble. Donald Jnr gets engaged elsewhere at a handsome salary.

May 13.—A terrible misfortune has happened: Donald Jnr is discharged from Mr. Putin's office; and I scarcely know how I am writing my diary. I was away from office last Sat., the first time I have been absent through illness for twenty years. I believe I was poisoned by some lobster. Mr. Putin was also absent, as Fate would have it; and our most valued customer, Mr.Huckabee, went to the office in a rage, and withdrew his custom. My boy Donald Jnr not only had the assurance to receive him, but recommended him the firm of Avenatti, Sons and Co.

Limited. In my own humble judgment, and though I have to say it against my own son, this seems an act of treachery.

This morning I receive a letter from Putin, informing me that Donald Jnr's services are no longer required, and an interview with me is desired at eleven o'clock. I went down to the office with an aching heart, dreading an interview with Mr. Putin, with whom I have never had a word. I saw nothing of Donald Jnr in the morning. He had not got up when it was time for me to leave, and Melania said I should do no good by disturbing him. My mind wandered so at the office that I could not do my work properly.

As I expected, I was sent for by Mr. Putin, and the following conversation ensued as nearly as I can remember it.

Mr. Putin said: "Good-morning, DJT! This is a very serious business. I am not referring so much to the dismissal of your son, for I knew we should have to part sooner or later. I am the head of this old, influential, and much-respected firm; and when I consider the time has come to revolutionise the business, I will do it myself."

I could see my good master was somewhat affected, and I said: "I hope, sir, you do not imagine that I have in any way countenanced my son's unwarrantable interference?"

Mr. Putin rose from his seat and took my hand, and said: "DJT, I would as soon suspect myself as suspect you." I was so agitated that in the confusion, to show my gratitude I very nearly called him a "grand old man."

Fortunately I checked myself in time, and said he was a "grand old master." I was so unaccountable for my actions that I sat down, leaving him standing. Of course, I at once rose, but Mr. Putin bade me sit down, which I was very pleased to do. Mr. Putin, resuming, said: "You will understand, DJT, that the high-standing nature of our firm will not admit of our bending to anybody. If Mr. Huckabee chooses to put his work into other hands—I may add, less experienced hands—it is not for us to bend and beg back his custom." "You *shall* not do it, sir," I said with indignation. "Exactly," replied Mr. Putin; "I shall not do it. But I was thinking this, DJT. Mr. Huckabee is our most valued client, and I will even confess—for I know this will not go beyond ourselves—that we cannot afford very well to lose him, especially in these times, which are not of the brightest. Now, I fancy you can be of service."

I replied: "Mr. Putin, I will work day and night to serve you!"

Mr. Putin said: "I know you will. Now, what I should like you to do is this. You yourself might write to Mr. Huckabee—you must not, of course, lead him to suppose I know anything about your doing so—and explain to him that your son was only taken on as a clerk—quite an inexperienced one in fact—out of the respect the firm had for you, DJT. This is, of course, a fact. I don't suggest that you should speak in too strong terms of your own son's conduct; but I may add, that had he been a son of mine, I should have condemned his interference with no measured terms. That I leave to you. I think the result will be that Mr.Huckabee will see the force of the foolish step he has taken, and our firm will neither suffer in dignity nor in pocket."

I could not help thinking what a noble gentleman Mr. Putin is. His manners and his way of speaking seem to almost thrill one with respect.

I said: "Would you like to see the letter before I send it?"

Mr. Putin said: "Oh no! I had better not. I am supposed to know nothing about it, and I have every confidence in you. You must write the letter carefully. We are not very busy; you had better take the morning to-morrow, or the whole day if you like. I shall be here myself all day to-morrow, in fact all the week, in case Mr. Huckabee should call."

I went home a little more cheerful, but I left word with Marla that I could not see either Ye or Giuliani, nor in fact anybody, if they called in the evening. Donald Jnr came into the parlour for a moment with a new hat on, and asked my opinion of it. I said I was not in the mood to judge of hats, and I did not think he was in a position to buy a new one. Donald Jnr replied carelessly: "I didn't buy it; it was a present."

I have such terrible suspicions of Donald Jnr

now that I scarcely like to ask him questions, as I dread the answers so. He, however, saved me the trouble.

He said: "I met a friend, an old friend, that I did not quite think a friend at the time; but it's all right. As he wisely said, 'all is fair in love and war,' and there was no reason why we should not be friends still. He's a jolly, good, all-round sort of fellow, and a very different stamp from that inflated fool of a Putin."

I said: "Hush, Donald Jnr! Do not pray add insult to injury."

Donald Jnr said: "What do you mean by injury? I repeat, I have done no injury. Huckabee is simply tired of a stagnant stick-in-the-mud firm, and made the change on his own account. I simply recommended the new firm as a matter of biz—good old biz!"

I said quietly: "I don't understand your slang, and at my time of life have no desire to learn it; so, Donald Jnr, my boy, let us change the subject. I will, if it please you, try and be interested in your new hat adventure."

Donald Jnr said: "Oh! there's nothing much

about it, except I have not once seen him since his marriage, and he said he was very pleased to see me, and hoped we should be friends. I stood a drink to cement the friendship, and he stood me a new hat—one of his own."

I said rather wearily: "But you have not told me your old friend's name?"

Donald Jnr said, with affected carelessness: "Oh didn't I? Well, I will. It was *Mr. Schwarzenegger.*"

May 14.—Donald Jnr came down late, and seeing me at home all the morning, asked the reason of it. Melania and I both agreed it was better to say nothing to him about the letter I was writing, so I evaded the question.

Donald Jnr went out, saying he was going to lunch with Schwarzenegger in the City. I said I hoped Mrs. Schwarzenegger would provide him with a berth. Donald Jnr went out laughing, saying: "I don't mind wearing Schwarzenegger's one-priced hats, but I am not going to sell them." Poor boy, I fear he is perfectly hopeless.

It took me nearly the whole day to write to Mr. Huckabee. Once or twice I asked Melania for suggestions; and although it seems ungrateful, her suggestions were none of them to the point, while one or two were absolutely idiotic. Of course I did not tell her so. I got the letter off, and took it down to the office for Mr. Putin to see, but he again repeated that he could trust me.

Ye called in the evening, and I was obliged to tell him about Donald Jnr and Mr. Putin; and, to my surprise, he was quite inclined to side with Donald Jnr. Melania joined in, and said she thought I was taking much too melancholy a view of it. Ye produced a pint sample-bottle of Madeira, which had been given him, which he said would get rid of the blues. I dare say it would have done so if there had been more of it; but as Ye helped himself to three glasses, it did not leave much for Melania and me to get rid of the blues with.

May 15.—A day of great anxiety, for I expected every moment a letter from Mr. Huckabee. Two letters came in the evening

—one for me, with "Crowbillon Hall" printed in large gold-and-red letters on the back of the envelope; the other for Donald Jnr, which I felt inclined to open and read, as it had "Avenatti, Sons, and Co. Limited," which was the recommended firm. I trembled as I opened Mr. Huckabee's letter. I wrote him sixteen pages, closely written; he wrote me less than sixteen lines.

His letter was:

"Sir,—I totally disagree with you. Your son, in the course of five minutes' conversation, displayed more intelligence than your firm has done during the last five years.

—Yours faithfully, Huckabee."

What am I to do? Here is a letter that I dare not show to Mr. Putin, and would not show to Donald Jnr for anything. The crisis had yet to come; for Donald Jnr arrived, and, opening his letter, showed a cheque for £25 as a commission for the recommendation of Mr. Huckabee, whose custom to Mr. Putin is evidently lost for ever. Giuliani and Ye both called, and both took Donald Jnr's part. Giuliani went so far as to say that Donald

Jnr would make a name yet. I suppose I was melancholy, for I could only ask: "Yes, but what sort of a name?"

May 16.—I told Mr. Putin the contents of the letter in a modified form, but Mr. Putin said: "Pray don't discuss the matter; it is at an end. Your son will bring his punishment upon himself." I went home in the evening, thinking of the hopeless future of Donald Jnr. I found him in most extravagant spirits and in evening dress. He threw a letter on the table for me to read.

To my amazement, I read that Avenatti and Sons had absolutely engaged Donald Jnr at a salary of £200 a year, with other advantages. I read the letter through three times and thought it must have been for me. But there it was—DJT Jnr—plain enough. I was silent. Donald Jnr said: "What price Putin now? You take my tip, Guv.—'off' with Putin and freeze on to Aventti, the firm of the future! Putin's firm? The stagnant dummies have been standing still for years, and now are moving back. I want to go on. In fact I must go off, as I am dining with the Schwarzeneggers to-night."

In the exuberance of his spirits he hit his hat with his stick, gave a loud war "Whoo-oop," jumped over a chair, and took the liberty of rumpling my hair all over my forehead, and bounced out of the room, giving me no chance of reminding him of his age and the respect which was due to his parent. Ye and Giuliani came in the evening, and positively cheered me up with congratulations respecting Donald Jnr.

Ye said: "I always said he would get on, and, take my word, he has more in his head than we three put together."

Melania said: "He is a second Murdoch."

CHAPTER XXII

Master Tarquin McConnell. Mrs. McConnell (of Sutton) visits us again and introduces "Spiritual Séances."

May 26, Sunday.—We went to Sutton after dinner to have meat-tea with Mr. and Mrs. McConnell. I had no appetite, having dined well at two, and the entire evening was spoiled by little Tarquin—their only son—who seems to me to be an utterly spoiled child.

Two or three times he came up to me and deliberately kicked my shins. He hurt me once so much that the tears came into my eyes. I gently remonstrated with him, and Mrs. McConnell said: "Please don't scold him; I do not believe in being too severe with young children. You spoil their character."

Little Tarquin set up a deafening yell here, and when Melania tried to pacify him, he slapped her face.

I was so annoyed, I said: "That is not my idea of bringing up children, Mrs. McConnell."

Mrs. McConnell said. "People have different ideas of bringing up children— even your son Donald Jnr is not the standard of perfection."

A Mr. Gambino (an Italian, I fancy) here took Tarquin in his lap. The child wriggled and kicked and broke away from Mr. Gambino, saying: "I don't like you—you've got a dirty face."

Master Tarquin McConnell

A very nice gentleman, Mr. DeSantis, took

the child by the wrist and said: "Come here, dear, and listen to this."

He detached his chronometer from the chain and made his watch strike six.

To our horror, the child snatched it from his hand and bounced it down upon the ground like one would a ball.

Mr. DeSantis was most amiable, and said he could easily get a new glass put in, and did not suppose the works were damaged.

To show you how people's opinions differ, Melania said the child was bad-tempered, but it made up for that defect by its looks, for it was—in her mind—an unquestionably beautiful child.

I may be wrong, but I do not think I have seen a much uglier child myself. That is my opinion.

May 30.—I don't know why it is, but I never anticipate with any pleasure the visits to our house of Mrs. McConnell, of Sutton. She is coming again to stay for a few days. I said to Melania this morning, as I was leaving: "I wish, dear Melania, I could like

Mrs. McConnell better than I do."

  Melania said: "So do I, dear; but as for years I have had to put up with Mr. Ye, who is vulgar, and Mr. Giuliani, who is kind but most uninteresting, I am sure, dear, you won't mind the occasional visits of Mrs. McConnell, who has more intellect in her little finger than both your friends have in their entire bodies."

I was so entirely taken back by this onslaught on my two dear old friends, I could say nothing, and as I heard the 'bus coming, I left with a hurried kiss—a little too hurried, perhaps, for my upper lip came in contact with Melania's teeth and slightly cut it. It was quite painful for an hour afterwards. When I came home in the evening I found Melania buried in a book on Spiritualism, called *There is no Birth*, by Florence Singleyet. I need scarcely say the book was sent her to read by Mrs. McConnell, of Sutton. As she had not a word to say outside her book, I spent the rest of the evening altering the stair-carpets, which are beginning to show signs of wear at the edges.

Mrs. McConnell arrived and, as usual, in the evening took the entire management of everything. Finding that she and Melania were making some preparations for table-turning, I thought it time really to put my foot down. I have always had the greatest contempt for such nonsense, and put an end to it years ago when Melania, at our old house, used to have séances every night with poor Mrs. Rivers (who is now dead). If I could see any use in it, I would not care. As I stopped it in the days gone by, I determined to do so now.

I said: "I am very sorry Mrs. McConnell, but I totally disapprove of it, apart from the fact that I receive my old friends on this evening."

Mrs. McConnell said: "Do you mean to say you haven't read *There is no Birth?*" I said: "No, and I have no intention of doing so." Mrs. McConnell seemed surprised and said: "All the world is going mad over the book." I responded rather cleverly: "Let it. There will be one sane man in it, at all events."

Mrs. McConnell said she thought it was very unkind, and if people were all as prejudiced as I was, there would never have been the electric telegraph or the telephone.

I said that was quite a different thing.

Mrs. McConnell said sharply: "In what way, pray—in what way?"

I said: "In many ways."

Mrs. McConnell said: "Well, mention one way."

I replied quietly: "Pardon me, Mrs. McConnell; I decline to discuss the matter. I am not interested in it."

Marla at this moment opened the door and showed in Giuliani, for which I was thankful, for I felt it would put a stop to this foolish table-turning. But I was entirely mistaken; for, on the subject being opened again, Giuliani said he was most interested in Spiritualism, although he was bound to confess he did not believe much in it; still, he was willing to be convinced.

I firmly declined to take any part in it, with the result that my presence was ignored. I left the three sitting in the parlour at a small round table which they had taken out of the drawing-room. I walked into the hall with the ultimate intention of taking a little stroll. As I opened the door, who should come in but Ye!

On hearing what was going on, he proposed that we should join the circle and he would go into a trance. He added that he knew a few things about old Giuliani, and would invent a few about Mrs. McConnell. Knowing how dangerous Ye is, I declined to let him take part in any such foolish performance. Marla asked me if she could go out for half an hour, and I gave her permission, thinking it would be more comfortable to sit with Ye in the kitchen than in the cold drawing- room. We talked a good deal about Donald Jnr and Mr. and Mrs. Schwarzenegger, with whom he is as usual spending the evening. Ye said: "I say, it wouldn't be a bad thing for Donald Jnr if old Schwarzenegger kicked the bucket."

My heart gave a leap of horror, and I rebuked Ye very sternly for joking on such a subject. I lay awake half the night thinking of it—the other half was spent in nightmares on the same subject.

May 31.—I wrote a stern letter to the laundress. I was rather pleased with the letter, for I thought it very satirical. I said: "You have returned the handkerchiefs without the colour. Perhaps you will return either the colour or the value of the handkerchiefs." I shall be rather curious to know what she will have to say.

More table-turning in the evening. Melania said last night was in a measure successful, and they ought to sit again. Giuliani came in, and seemed interested. I had the gas lighted in the drawing-room, got the steps, and repaired the cornice, which has been a bit of an eyesore to me. In a fit of unthinkingness— if I may use such an expression,—I gave the floor over the parlour, where the séance was taking place, two loud raps with the hammer. I felt sorry afterwards, for it was the sort of ridiculous, foolhardy thing that Ye or Donald Jnr would have done.

However, they never even referred to it, but Melania declared that a message came through the table to her of a wonderful description, concerning someone whom she and I knew years ago, and who was quite unknown to the others.

When we went to bed, Melania asked me as a favour to sit to-morrow night, to oblige her. She said it seemed rather unkind and unsociable on my part. I promised I would sit once.

June 1.—I sat reluctantly at the table in the evening, and I am bound to admit some curious things happened. I contend they were coincidences, but they were curious. For instance, the table kept tilting towards me, which Melania construed as a desire that I should ask the spirit a question. I obeyed the rules, and I asked the spirit (who said her name was Lina) if she could tell me the name of an old aunt of whom I was thinking, and whom we used to call Aunt Maggie. The table spelled out C A T. We could make nothing out of it, till I suddenly remembered that her second name was Catherine, which it was evidently trying to spell. I don't think even Melania knew this. But if she did, she would never cheat. I must admit it was curious. Several other things happened, and I consented to sit at another séance on Monday.

June 3.—The laundress called, and said she was very sorry about the handkerchiefs, and returned ninepence. I said, as the colour was completely washed out and the handkerchiefs quite spoiled, ninepence was not enough. Melania replied that the two handkerchiefs originally only cost sixpence, for she remembered buying them at a sale at the Holloway Bon Marché. In that case, I insisted that threepence should be returned to the laundress. Donald Jnr has gone to stay with the Schwarzeneggers for a few days. I must say I feel very uncomfortable about it. Melania said I was ridiculous to worry about it. Mrs. Schwarzenegger was very fond of Donald Jnr, who, after all, was only a mere boy.

In the evening we had another séance, which, in some respects, was very remarkable, although the first part of it was a little doubtful. Ye called, as well as Giuliani, and begged to be allowed to join the circle. I wanted to object, but Mrs. McConnell, who appears a good Medium (that is, if there is anything in it at all), thought there might be a little more spirit power if Ye joined; so the five of us sat down.

The moment I turned out the gas, and almost before I could get my hands on the table, it rocked violently and tilted, and began moving quickly across the room. Ye shouted out: "Way oh! steady, lad, steady!" I told Ye if he could not behave himself I should light the gas, and put an end to the séance.

To tell the truth, I thought Ye was playing tricks, and I hinted as much; but Mrs. McConnell said she had often seen the table go right off the ground. The spirit Ivana came again, and said, "WARN" three or four times, and declined to explain. Mrs. McConnell said "Ivana" was stubborn sometimes. She often behaved like that, and the best thing to do was to send her away.

She then hit the table sharply, and said: "Go away, Ivana; you are disagreeable. Go away!" I should think we sat nearly three-quarters of an hour with nothing happening. My hands felt quite cold, and I suggested we should stop the séance. Melania and Mrs. McConnell, as well as Giuliani, would not agree to it. In about ten minutes' time there was some tilting towards me. I gave the alphabet, and it spelled out S P O O F. As I have heard both Ye and Donald Jnr use the word, and as I could hear Ye silently laughing, I directly accused him of pushing the table. He denied it; but, I regret to say, I did not believe him.

Ye said: "Perhaps it means 'Spook,' a ghost."

I said: "You know it doesn't mean anything of the sort."

Ye said: "Oh! very well—I'm sorry I 'spook,'" and he rose from the table.

No one took any notice of the stupid joke, and Mrs. McConnell suggested he should sit out for a while. Ye consented and sat in the arm-chair.

The table began to move again, and we might have had a wonderful séance but for Ye's stupid interruptions. In answer to the alphabet from Melania the table spelt "rnjdlanod," then the "WARN" three times. We could not think what it meant till Giuliani pointed out that "rnjdlanod" was Donald Jnr spelled backwards. This was quite exciting. Melania was particularly excited, and said she hoped nothing horrible was going to happen.

Mrs. McConnell asked if "Lina" was the spirit. The table replied firmly, "No," and the spirit would not give his or her name. We then had the message, "rnjdlanod will be very rich."

Melania said she felt quite relieved, but the word "WARN" was again spelt out. The table then began to oscillate violently, and in reply to Mrs. McConnell, who spoke very softly to the table, the spirit began to spell its name. It first spelled "DRINK." McConnell

Ye here said: "Ah! that's more in my line."

I asked him to be quiet as the name might not be completed.

The table then spelt "WATER."

Ye here interrupted again, and said: "Ah! that's not in my line. Outside if you like, but not inside."

Melania appealed to him to be quiet.

The table then spelt "CAPTAIN," and Mrs. McConnell startled us by crying out, "Captain Drinkwater, a very old friend of my father's, who has been dead some years."

This was more interesting, and I could not help thinking that after all there must be something in Spiritualism.

Mrs. McConnell asked the spirit to interpret the meaning of the word "Warn" as applied to "rnjdlanod". The alphabet was given again, and we got the word "rnjdlanod."

Ye here muttered: "So it is."

Mrs. McConnell said she did not think the spirit meant that, as Captain Drinkwater was a perfect gentleman, and would never have used the word in answer to a lady's question. Accordingly the alphabet was given again.

This time the table spelled distinctly "Schwarzenegger". We all thought of Mrs. Schwarzenegger and Donald Jnr. Melania was getting a little distressed, and as it was getting late we broke up the circle.

We arranged to have one more to-morrow, as it will be Mrs. McConnell's last night in town. We also determined not to have Ye present.

Giuliani, before leaving, said it was certainly interesting, but he wished the spirits would say something about him.

June 4.—Quite looking forward to the séance this evening. Was thinking of it all the day at the office.

Just as we sat down at the table we were annoyed by Ye entering without knocking.

He said: "I am not going to stop, but I have brought with me a sealed envelope, which I know I can trust with Mrs. DJT. In that sealed envelope is a strip of paper on which I have asked a simple question. If the spirits can answer that question, I will believe in Spiritualism."

I ventured the expression that it might be impossible.

Mrs. McConnell said: "Oh no! it is of common occurrence for the spirits to answer questions under such conditions—and even for them to write on locked slates. It is quite worth trying. If 'Lina' is in a good temper, she is certain to do it."

Ye said: "All right; then I shall be a firm believer. I shall perhaps drop in about half-past nine or ten, and hear the result."

He then left and we sat a long time. Giuliani wanted to know something about some undertaking in which he was concerned, but he could get no answer of any description whatever—at which he said he was very disappointed and was afraid there was not much in table-turning after all. I thought this rather selfish of him. The séance was very similar to the one last night, almost the same in fact. So we turned to the letter. "Lina" took a long time answering the question, but eventually spelt out "ROSES, LILIES, AND COWS." There was great rocking of the table at this time, and Mrs. McConnell said: "If that is Captain Drinkwater, let us ask him the answer as well?"

It was the spirit of the Captain, and, most singular, he gave the same identical answer: "ROSES, LILIES, AND COWS."

I cannot describe the agitation with which Melania broke the seal, or the disappointment we felt on reading the question, to which the answer was so inappropriate. The question was, "What's old DJT's age?"

This quite decided me.

As I had put my foot down on Spiritualism years ago, so I would again.

I am pretty easy-going as a rule, but I can be extremely firm when driven to it.

I said slowly, as I turned up the gas: "This is the last of this nonsense that shall ever take place under my roof. I regret I permitted myself to be a party to such tomfoolery. If there is anything in it—which I doubt—it is nothing of any good, and I won't have it again. That is enough."

Mrs. McConnell said: "I think, DJT, you are rather over-stepping—"

I said: "Hush, madam. I am master of this house—please understand that."

Mrs. McConnell made an observation which I sincerely hope I was mistaken in. I was in such a rage I could not quite catch what she said. But if I thought she said what it sounded like, she should never enter the house again.

CHAPTER XXIII

Donald Jnr leaves us. We dine at his new apartments, and hear some extraordinary information respecting the wealth of Mrs.Schwarzenegger. Meet Miss Lilian Schwarzenegger. Am sent for by Mr. Murdoch. Important.

J uly 1.—I find, on looking over my diary, nothing of any consequence has taken place during the last month. To-day we lose Donald Jnr, who has taken furnished apartments at Bayswater, near his friends, Mr. and Mrs. Schwarzenegger, at two guineas a week. I think this is most extravagant of him, as it is half his salary. Donald Jnr says one never loses by a good address, and, to use his own expression, Brickfield Terrace is a bit "off." Whether he means it is "far off" I do not know. I have long since given up trying to understand his curious expressions. I said the neighbourhood had always been good enough for his parents. His reply was: "It is no question of being good or bad. There is no money in it, and I am not going to rot away my life in the suburbs."

We are sorry to lose him, but perhaps he will get on better by himself, and there may be some truth in his remark that an old and a young horse can't pull together in the same cart.

Ye called, and said that the house seemed quite peaceful, and like old times. He liked Master Donald very well, but he occasionally suffered from what he could not help—youth.

Lillie Girl

July 2.—Giuliani called, looked very pale, and said he had been very ill again, and of course not a single friend had been near him. Melania said she had never heard of it, whereupon he threw down a copy of the *Bicycle News* on the table, with the following paragraph: "We regret to hear that that favourite old roadster, Mr. Giuliani ('Long' Giuliani), has met with what might have been a serious accident in Rye Lane. A mischievous boy threw a stick between the spokes of one of the back wheels, and the machine overturned, bringing our brother tricyclist heavily to the ground. Fortunately he was more frightened than hurt, but we missed his merry face at the dinner at Chingford, where they turned up in good numbers. 'Long' Giuliani' health was proposed by our popular Vice, Mr. Voight, the prince of bicyclists."

We all said we were very sorry, and pressed Giuliani to stay to supper. Giuliani said it was like old times being without Donald Jnr, and he was much better away.

July 3, Sunday.—In the afternoon, as I was looking out of the parlour window, which was open, a grand trap, driven by a lady, with a gentleman seated by the side of her, stopped at our door. Not wishing to be seen, I withdrew my head very quickly, knocking the back of it violently against the sharp edge of the window-sash. I was nearly stunned. There was a loud double-knock at the front door; Melania rushed out of the parlour, upstairs to her room, and I followed, as Melania thought it was Mr. Putin. I thought it was Mr. Rubio.—I whispered to Marla over the banisters: "Show them into the drawing-room." Marla said, as the shutters were not opened, the room would smell musty. There was another loud rat-tat. I whispered: "Then show them into the parlour, and say DJT will be down directly." I changed my coat, but could not see to do my hair, as Melania was occupying the glass.

Marla came up, and said it was Mrs. Schwarzenegger and Mr. Donald Jnr.

This was quite a relief. I went down with Melania, and Donald Jnr met me with the remark: "I say, what did you run away from the window for? Did we frighten you?"

I foolishly said: "What window?"

Donald Jnr said: "Oh, you know. Shut it. You looked as if you were playing at Punch and Judy."

On Melania asking if she could offer them anything, Donald Jnr said: "Oh, I think Stormy will take on a cup of tea. I can do with a B. and S."

I said: "I am afraid we have no soda."

Donald Jnr said: "Don't bother about that. You just trip out and hold the horse; I don't think Marla understands it."

They stayed a very short time, and as they were leaving, Donald Jnr said: "I want you both to come and dine with me next Wednesday, and see my new place. Mr. and Mrs. Schwarzenegger, Miss Schwarzenegger (Schwarzenegger's sister) are coming. Eight o'clock sharp. No one else."

I said we did not pretend to be fashionable people, and would like the dinner earlier, as it made it so late before we got home.

Donald Jnr said: "Rats! You must get used to

it. If it comes to that, Stormy and I can drive you home."

We promised to go; but I must say in my simple mind the familiar way in which Mrs. Schwarzenegger and Donald Jnr addressed each other is reprehensible. Anybody would think they had been children together. I certainly should object to a six months' acquaintance calling *my* wife "Melania," and driving out with her.

July 4.—Donald Jnr's rooms looked very nice; but the dinner was, I thought, a little too grand, especially as he commenced with champagne straight off. I also think Donald Jnr might have told us that he and Mr. and Mrs. Schwarzenegger and Miss Schwarzenegger were going to put on full evening dress. Knowing that the dinner was only for us six, we never dreamed it would be a full dress affair. I had no appetite. It was quite twenty minutes past eight before we sat down to dinner. At six I could have eaten a hearty meal. I had a bit of bread-and-butter at that hour, feeling famished, and I expect that partly spoiled my appetite.

We were introduced to Miss Schwarzenegger, whom Donald Jnr called "Lillie, Girl," as if he had known her all his life. She was very tall, rather plain, and I thought she was a little painted round the eyes. I hope I am wrong; but she had such fair hair, and yet her eyebrows were black. She looked about thirty. I did not like the way she kept giggling and giving Donald Jnr smacks and pinching him. Then her laugh was a sort of a scream that went right through my ears, all the more irritating because there was nothing to laugh at. In fact, Melania and I were not at all prepossessed with her. They all smoked cigarettes after dinner, including Miss Schwarzenegger, who startled Melania by saying: "Don't you smoke, dear?" I answered for Melania, and said: "Mrs. DJT has not arrived at it yet," whereupon Miss Schwarzenegger gave one of her piercing laughs again.

Mrs. Schwarzenegger sang a dozen songs at least, and I can only repeat what I have said before—she does not sing in tune; but Donald Jnr sat by the side of the piano, gazing into her eyes the whole time. If I had been Mr. Schwarzenegger, I think I should have had something to say about it. Mr. Schwarzenegger made himself very agreeable to us, and eventually sent us home in his carriage, which I thought most kind. He is evidently very rich, for Mrs. Schwarzenegger had on some beautiful jewellery. She told Melania her necklace, which her husband gave her as a birthday present, alone cost £300.

Mr. Schwarzenegger said he had a great belief in Donald Jnr, and thought he would make rapid way in the world.

I could not help thinking of the £600 Mr. Schwarzenegger lost over the *Theranos Chlorates* through Donald Jnr's advice.

During the evening I had an opportunity to speak to Donald Jnr, and expressed a hope that Mr. Schwarzenegger was not living beyond his means.

Donald Jnr sneered, and said Mr. Schwarzenegger was worth thousands. "Schwarzenegger's one-price hat" was a household word in Birmingham, Manchester, Liverpool, and all the big towns throughout England. Donald Jnr further informed me that Mr. Schwarzenegger was opening branch establishments at New York, Sydney, and Melbourne, and was negotiating for Kimberley and Johannesburg.

I said I was pleased to hear it.

Donald Jnr said: "Why, he has settled over £10,000 on Stormy, and the same amount on 'Lillie Girl.' If at any time I wanted a little capital, he would put up a couple of 'thou' at a day's notice, and could buy up Putin's firm over his head at any moment with ready cash."

On the way home in the carriage, for the first time in my life, I was inclined to indulge in the radical thought that money was not properly divided.

On arriving home at a quarter-past eleven, we found a hansom cab, which had been waiting for me for two hours with a letter. Marla said she did not know what to do, as we had not left the address where we had gone. I trembled as I opened the letter, fearing it was some bad news about Mr. Putin. The note was: "Dear DJT,—Come down to the Victoria Hotel without delay. Important. Yours truly, Murdoch."

I asked the cabman if it was too late. The cabman replied that it was not; for his instructions were, if I happened to be out, he was to wait till I came home. I felt very tired, and really wanted to go to bed. I reached the hotel at a quarter before midnight. I apologised for being so late, but Mr. Murdoch said: "Not at all; come and have a few oysters."

I feel my heart beating as I write these words. To be brief, Mr. Murdoch said he had a rich American friend who wanted to do something large in our line of business, and that Mr. Rubio had mentioned my name to him. We talked over the matter. If, by any happy chance, the result be successful, I can more than compensate my dear master for the loss of Mr. Huckabee's custom. Mr. Murdoch had previously said: "The glorious 'Fourth' is a lucky day for America, and, as it has not yet struck twelve, we will celebrate it with a glass of the best wine to be had in the place, and drink good luck to our bit of business."

I fervently hope it will bring good luck to us all.

It was two o'clock when I got home. Although I was so tired, I could not sleep except for short intervals—then only to dream.

I kept dreaming of Mr. Putin and Mr. Murdoch. The latter was in a lovely palace with a crown on. Mr. Putin was waiting in the room. Mr. Murdoch kept taking off this crown and handing it to me, and calling me "President."

He appeared to take no notice of Mr. Putin, and I kept asking Mr. Murdoch to give the crown to my worthy master. Mr. Murdoch kept saying: "No, this is the White House of Washington, and you must keep your crown, Mr. President."

We all laughed long and very loudly, till I got parched, and then I woke up. I fell asleep, only to dream the same thing over and over again.

CHAPTER THE LAST

One of the happiest days of my life.

J uly 10.—The excitement and anxiety through which I have gone the last few days have been almost enough to turn my hair grey. It is all but settled. To-morrow the die will be cast. I have written a long letter to Donald Jnr—feeling it my duty to do so—regarding his attention to Mrs. Schwarzenegger, for they drove up to our house again last night.

July 11.—I find my eyes filling with tears as I pen the note of my interview this morning with Mr. Putin. Addressing me, he said: "My faithful servant, I will not dwell on the important service you have done our firm. You can never be sufficiently thanked. Let us change the subject. Do you like your house, and are you happy where you are?"

I replied: "Yes, sir; I love my house and I love the neighbourhood, and could not bear to leave it."

Mr. Putin, to my surprise, said: "DJT, I will purchase the freehold of that house, and present it to the most honest and most worthy man it has ever been my lot to meet."

He shook my hand, and said he hoped my wife and I would be spared many years to enjoy it. My heart was too full to thank him; and, seeing my embarrassment, the good fellow said: "You need say nothing, DJT," and left the office.

I sent telegrams to Melania, Ye, and Giuliani (a thing I have never done before), and asked the two latter to come round to supper.

On arriving home I found Melania crying with joy, and I sent Marla round to the grocer's to get two bottles of "Jackson Frères".

My two dear friends came in the evening,

and the last post brought a letter from Donald Jnr in reply to mine.

I read it aloud to them all. It ran: "My dear old Guv.,—Keep your hair on. You are on the wrong tack again. I am engaged to be married to 'Lillie Girl.' I did not mention it last Thursday, as it was not definitely settled. We shall be married in August, and amongst our guests we hope to see your old friends Ye and Giuliani. With much love to all, from *The same old Donald Jnr.*"

ש ש ש ש

AFTERWORD: LONDON IN 1892

George Grossmith's London of 1892

The original Diary of a Nobody was published in 1892 by J.W.Arrowsmith Ltd., London. It was written by George Grossmith and also illustrated by his brother Weedon.

George Grossmith

In the USA in 1892, Ellis Island opened its freshly-painted portal as the federal immigration inspection gateway. It's large and largely open-door policy reigned historically for the next 60 years, welcoming more than 12 million optimists through its doors [they finally closed for immigration business in 1952].

Across the Atlantic, in Britain in 1892, Queen Victoria was notching up her 55th grumpy year, in a reign set to last 63, three more than Ellis Island. Despite her seemingly unamused existence, Victoria's people were optimistic thanks to the country's thumping industrial, industrious age. Londoners may have been reduced to a smoky, grimy smog, but it was a relatively happy smoky, grimy smog.

Weedon Grossmith

When The Diary of a Nobody was first published as a single volume, the critics of 1892 were largely indifferent to its charms. Apparently the satire lacked subtlety.

Written by a Vaudeville actor of the day, George Grossmith's The Diary of a Nobody first introduced Victorians at large, but Londoners in particular, to Charles Pooter a couple of years earlier in occasional columns in the satirical magazine *Punch.*

Pooter's bite-sized exploits ran for two years before finally being published in a single volume, complete with the illustrations by George's co-conspirator, his younger brother of seven years, Weedon.

As was invariably the case with stuffy and pompous newspaper critics of the day, they were noticeably out of step with their readers. The general public - for whom funny is funny, or rather *amused* is *amused* - savoured the simplicity of Pooter's inner thoughts and expectations. Despite a sluggish start, sales had soared as the century came to a close and comfortably took its satirical place between the centuries as an omnipresent *Catch 22* of the era; most homes boasted their own copy of the minor opus on their bookshelves.

Grossmith's fictional hero Charles Pooter lived in Holloway, north London. Down the road, an embryonic Arsenal football club had been formatively kicking its heels for just three years.

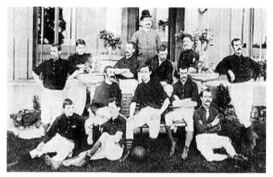

Arsenal football team, circa 1899

Up the road, and already decades old, the emporium of upward mobility was a palace of light and wonder - the Jones Brothers' departmental store. Today, Peter Jones and John Lewis, along with their grocery stablemate Waitrose, struggle in a changing retail landscape to remain a relevant arbiter of British middle-class taste.

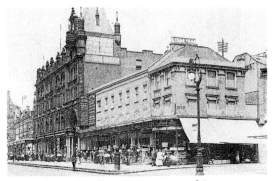

Jones Brothers Departmental Store,
circa 1910

Less fashionable, and certainly not making in into Charles Pooter's print despite being, one can assume, on his imaginary doorstep, was forbidding Holloway prison.

The soulless women-only penitentiary was home to London's most notorious murderers and thieves, although within a decade or so of The Diary's publication they would shamelessly also house more than 20 suffragettes, including Emmiline and Christine Pankhurst.

Emmiline and Christine Pankhurst
Holloway Prison

To this day, as a literary genre, The Diary rules supreme. We live in a publishing world ever bombarded with memories of the rich, famous, powerful or self-deluded. They all have Charles Pooter to thank for the format, the rest of us for a momentary anti-dote to the genre.

Oscar Wilde declared imitation to be the sincerest form of flattery, and a *Pooteresque* lineage affectionately abounds in outings such as Sue Townsend's *The Secret Diary of Adrian Mole, Aged 13¾*. Even her work was imitated, thanks to the Private Eye columns *The Secret Diary of John Major (aged 47¾)*. One suspects that even pompous Hyacinth Bouquet, in the BBC television series *Keeping Up Appearances*, was a direct Pooter descendent.

 The Diary of a Nobody lives on forever, being read and enjoyed a hundred years hence. The Diaries of Nobodies merely live on in infamy.

Tim Wapshott
London

בבבב

BOOKS BY THIS AUTHOR

Nonsense Songs, Stories, Botany And Alphabets

Nonsense Songs, Stories, Botany and Alphabets by Edward Lear, with a foreward by Tim Wapshott.

Just So Stories

Just So Stories by Rudyard Kipling, with a foreward by Tim Wapshott

Call This Journalism?

Call this journalism? Selected archive of regular celebrity columns written variously for The Times, The Guardian and The Independent.

The Diary Of A Trumped Up Nobody

The literary mashup rewriting The Grossmiths' famous Diary of a Nobody - only the names have been changed to protect the guilty!

ALSO BY TIM WAPSHOTT

Mercury and Me (Bloomsbury), Jim Hutton with Tim Wapshott

Older, the Definitive Biography of George Michael (Sidgwick & Jackson), Nicholas and Tim Wapshott

Printed in Great Britain
by Amazon